A TRUSTED
FINANCIAL
ADVISOR

Secrets To Become A Trusted Financial Advisor Everyone Raves About
Copyright ©2018 Mark Purnell

All Rights Reserved. Printed in the U.S.A.
ISBN-13: 978-1986938945
ISBN-10: 1986938948

All rights reserved. This book or any portion thereof may not be reproduced or used in any manner whatsoever without the express written permission of the publisher, except for the use of brief quotations in a book review. The scanning, uploading, and distribution of this book via the Internet, or any other means, without the permission of the publisher is illegal and punishable by law.

The purchaser of this book is subject to the condition that he/she shall in no way resell it, nor any part of it, nor make copies of it to distribute freely.

This book is intended for educational and training purposes. Some names, characters, businesses, places, events and details of incidents have been changed to protect the privacy of individuals. Any resemblance to actual persons, living or dead, or actual events is purely coincidental and the author apologizes for any oversights and similarities to an individual or family.

The book reflects the author's present recollections of experiences over time. Some events have been compressed, and some dialogue has been recreated.

The author has tried to recreate events, locales and conversations from his memories of them. In order to maintain their anonymity in some instances he has changed the names of individuals and places. He may have also changed some identifying characteristics and details such as physical properties, occupations, places of residence, references and other events.

Although the author and publisher have made every effort to ensure that the referenced information in this book was correct at press time, the author and publisher do not assume and hereby disclaim any liability to any party for any loss, damage, or disruption caused by errors or omissions, whether such errors or omissions result from negligence, accident, or any other cause.

The author and publisher do not provide tax, legal or accounting advice. This book has been written for educational and training purposes only, and is not intended to provide, and should not be relied on for, tax, legal or accounting advice. The reader should consult their own tax, legal and accounting advisors before engaging in any transaction.

Publishing and Design:

Quantity sales. Special discounts are available on quantity purchases by corporations, associations, and others. For details, contact the publisher at the address above. Orders by U.S. trade book-stores and wholesalers.

Contact: 800-273-1625 | support@epicauthor.com | EpicAuthor.com

For more information about Mark Purnell or to book her for your next event or media interview, visit: MarkPurnell.net

SECRETS TO BECOME A TRUSTED FINANCIAL ADVISOR EVERYONE RAVES ABOUT

MARK W. PURNELL, CIMA

Dedication

I dedicate this book to
Yolanda Valentine and Ernest Purnell
My mother and father.

You have provided so much love, affection, encouragement, and prayers.

Your stewardship over the ancestral guidance and wisdom from

Amy Dundridge
Lucy Johnson
Rebecca Winston
Agatha Baul

Joseph Whittington Purnell
James Whittington Purnell
Louis Purnell
Ernest Purnell

has been one of your greatest gifts to me.

Acknowledgments

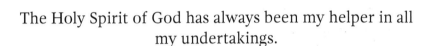

The Holy Spirit of God has always been my helper in all my undertakings.

I am totally grateful that through its ministry I have been able to do this work.

Through the power of the Holy Trinity:

God the Father
God the Son
and
God the Holy Spirit

I have been able to believe in my passions and pursue my dreams in ways that would not have been possible without the faith I have in God the Almighty.

Jehovah-Jireh "the LORD will provide."

Additional Acknowledgments

It has been a tremendous *growth experience* for me to complete this project. There are so many people to thank for their guidance, support, and advice.

To my son, Brandon, thanks for the love and support, the late-night reviews, and for asking the unanswered questions.

To Rose King, my best friend, and closest advisor, you encouraged me to start this journey. You helped me stay on course and lead the efforts of the Facebook book launch team.

To my publisher, business coach and mentor and team, Trevor Crane and Ashley Peterson, you are simply amazing, and I appreciate your patience with me.

To Jon Low, our collaborative sessions were so valuable, and you are a gifted writing coach and communicator. Along with editor Hilary Jastram, you both contributed so much to this project and helped me see it through to the end.

Table of Contents

Acknowledgments vi
Foreword xv
Bonus xix
Introduction 1

SECTION I: The Opportunity You Have
    CH 1: Your Big Opportunity In A Fiercely
            Competitive Market 11
    CH 2: What High-Net-Worth Clients Really Want 33
    CH 3: The Formula For A Profitable Practice 47

SECTION II: Maximize Gain & Minimize Pain
    CH 4: Get Known Without Spending A Fortune 69
    CH 5: Grow Your Business Without Burning Out 83

SECTION III: Secure Clients For Life
    CH 6: A Fast Track To Rapid Growth 107
    CH 7: A Step-By-Step Process To Secure
            High-Net-Wealth Clients 121

SECTION IV: Thrill Your Clients
    CH 8: Become Your Client's Point Of Power 131
    CH 9: How To Thrill Your Clients Time After Time 151

SECTION V: Built To Last
    CH 10: Secure Hidden Profit Streams That Are
             Right Under Your Nose 177
    CH 11: The Success Mindset Every Trusted
             Advisor Needs 189

Appendix 205
About Mark Purnell 211

Raving Fans

When forming a planning committee for a substantial post-retirement project I sought Mark as a coach, mentor and advisory network thought leader and strategist.

Mark is an effective and successful business leader, and in this book, he shares his win/win strategies in team formation and achieving positive and measurable outcomes.

I have personally watched Mark over the last 30 years and I love Mark for many reasons: his generous nature, his capacity to bring out the best in people and how he advocates for improving communities.

Michael Kern
Principle Engineer
Johnson Controls

Throughout this read, Mark provides invaluable advice to help financial advisory firms effectively move from a growth to an expansion phase. Within each chapter, Mark supports his advice with data and real-life examples from his 30+ years of financial advisory experience.

My personal favorite chapter is, "The Formula For A Profitable Practice" as this gives a peek behind the curtains of an income statement of a successful advisory practice along with guidance on how to tweak revenue and expense expectations based on the size of a firm.

Secrets to Become a Trusted Financial Advisor Everyone Raves About is a must-read for any current or prospective financial advisor who wants to plan for success over the next decade.

Joshua Wheeler, CPA, CIA

"Just finished the book and I'm blown away! Chapter 10 is the most useful chapter to me,

"Securing Hidden Profit Streams That Are Right Under Your Nose." I read "Get Known Without Spending A Fortune" twice and found it very useful and thought-provoking... Great book!"

James H. Coleman
First Vice President-Investments
The Coleman Gribben Group
Wells Fargo Advisors

"Mark has a long history of success in helping clients achieve their investment goals. What makes Mark unique is his style of success built upon a strong foundation of truly caring for his clients and thus helping them unlock a path to achieving their financial dreams. He clearly has a compelling story to tell in helping other advisors learn firsthand about his client-centric experiences."

Barry Sullivan
Sullivan & Associates Wealth Management, LLC

I've known Mark for more than 20 years. He is a brilliant mind. Mark has a way of making the complex simple. Every time that I have spoken with him, I have learned something new. What makes Mark special is that he is into the "helping people" business and this book focuses on client-centered strategies that will help any advisor who reads it. I read Chapter 10 "Secure Hidden Profit Streams That Are Right Under Your Nose" with great interest. This is a very brilliant way to address the lower end of one's book. I have always had a weird feeling about getting rid of the bottom 10%.

James L. Smith
Senior Financial Advisor
Wells Fargo Advisors Financial Network

Foreword

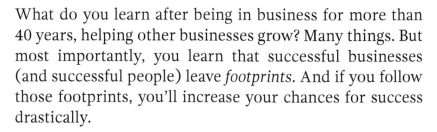

What do you learn after being in business for more than 40 years, helping other businesses grow? Many things. But most importantly, you learn that successful businesses (and successful people) leave *footprints*. And if you follow those footprints, you'll increase your chances for success drastically.

My name is Bill Good, and I'm the CEO of Bill Good Marketing. For decades we have specialized in teaching advisors how to do client marketing, prospecting, and build a million-dollar practice using our CRM-based system.

When people read "CRM-based system," one could be misled to believe that we forget about the people. *Nothing could be further from the truth.*

At the core of every successful business are people; those who work for and with the business, those who are affiliated with the business, and the customers. Mark is very much about the people; serving their needs, aligning their interests, and making sure everyone wins (you, included).

In this book, Mark Purnell shares timeless principles for advisors who want to take their advisory business to

FOREWORD

the next level. He covers vast ground in an engaging and conversational manner, from exploring the latest trends in the industry, sharing proven principles of building a profitable and sustainable business, to the finer points of human psychology that everyone ought to know if you are interacting with people.

This book's strength is unequivocally about aligning the interests and values of individuals and the wider community and doing so in such a way that you prosper, too, both in your practice and your personal life.

Bill Good
Author: *Hot Prospects: The Proven Prospecting System to Ramp Up Your Sales Career*
CEO, Bill Good Marketing

BONUS: Free Strategy Call

You can book your FREE strategy call with Mark Purnell, valued at $300. On that call, Mark will work with you to clarify your goals and assess your needs. This could be any one or more of the following:

- GAIN high-net-wealth clients without having to spend a fortune.
- Develop WINNING strategies for your clients that aren't based on "luck," and strategies that will thrill them time after time.
- Build and SUSTAIN your practice in the short term and for the long-run.
- Secure HIDDEN profit streams that are right under your nose.
- Be THE PREFERRED ADVISOR clients and other consultants in your community think of first whenever they have a want or need.
- Turn your competition and foes into raving FANS.
- BUILD and lead a winning team of advisors.
- Get MORE done in less time.

To book your free strategy session, go to: MarkPurnell.net/bonus

I look forward to working with you to gain the BEST of what life can offer!

—**Mark W. Purnell**, *CIMA*

INTRODUCTION

Hello!

MARK PURNELL HERE. I'M so glad this book is in your hands. Writing it is my way to give back to a profession that has been a blessing to me, my family, and my community. Before we start, I want to share a bit about myself, so you know exactly where I am coming from and what I'm about. And more importantly, what I'm <u>not</u> about.

Growing up, I didn't come from money. But I learned a lot about money over the years. I am the grandson of an elevator operator who moonlighted as a sandwich maker and part-time life insurance salesman. Fortunately for me, Pop Valentine taught me the security of building capital and storing value through a modest coin collection of his own.

Pop Valentine helped me lay my foundational understanding, and I built upon it over the course of my life. I have since spent my life studying and learning about

INTRODUCTION

money and sharing my experiences with other Family Stewards, so their families can fulfill their dreams and aspirations long after either of us stop coming to the breakfast table.

I've also been an entrepreneur and advisor since the age of 23 (I'm now 60). I have owned and operated entities in real estate, financial education, and financial services. Over the 33-years of my professional career, I have served clients in 34 states throughout the USA. Many are high-net-worth clients. And many didn't start out that way. But over the years, they eventually attained this status.

I have made a lot of money for clients over the course of my career. But more importantly, I have worked to align their interests with their money, helped them plan to live the life of their dreams, and sometimes, the life they never thought possible. In the last decade, I have provided over $400,000 to support philanthropic and charitable interests, benefitting the wider community.

Because of the deep understanding of the client's goals and objectives, rather than having anyone tell me what I "should" do or what I "must" do—clients and other advisors frequently ask me to tell them what *they* ought to do.

My secret sauce to success as an advisor is in this book. You don't have to go through decades of trial and error figuring it out. I've laid out the blueprint for you. But you will have to apply what you read and learn. The stuff I teach works...!

A TRUSTED FINANCIAL ADVISOR

> *"Despite not being an alumnus, Mark has fully committed himself to the betterment of our greater community through his volunteer service to the university. He has recognized the power of education for both the individual student as well as the urban public/private partnership. He is passionate, creative, and dedicated, and the university benefits greatly from his expertise and partnership..."*
>
> *—Jennifer Clearwater, CFRE*

Doing what I do, I have been blessed to accept my calling as an innovator, express my entrepreneurial spirit, and enjoy a life of realized dreams.

Some of these include:

- Provided unique insight and guidance through the tumultuous times of
    - Black Monday – the Stock Market Crash of 1987
    - Asian financial crisis 1997
    - Dot-Com Bubble, September 11 Attack, and Market Downturn 2000-2002
    - Financial Crisis of 2007 and the resulting Great Recession
- Enjoyed a practice that has allowed me to work with and learn from amazing clients and their families that have included:
    - National Basketball Association Hall of Famer, All Star and World Champions,
    - An internationally acclaimed landscape artist,

INTRODUCTION

- ○ Founders/owners of a nationally-known and recognized "Mega Franchise" and

- ○ Numerous corporate CEOs, business and community leaders.

- Lived and enjoyed a western Rocky Mountain lifestyle as a resident of Salt Lake City, UT and maintained an office in Milwaukee, WI,

- Celebrated and recognized overlooked heroes, both individuals and organizations that have made a positive impact on communities.

But the money and the material stuff aren't the only reasons I do what I do. People think the financial advisory profession is all about money. It's not. It's about friendship, integrity, and trust.

The work you do is about creating more *choices* for your clients, who, over time, will also become your friends. Through sound guidance, you can potentially help them retire with peace of mind, send their kids off to college, secure the home they have always wanted, and start businesses, so they can do what they love, as they support their charitable interests.

More to the heart of the matter, you'll also see people through some of their toughest challenges and transitions in life. From grieving loved ones, to finding new jobs after a redundancy, and dealing with divorces.

I love what I do because life is about contribution, to our family, loved ones, and those around us. I succeed because I put *their* needs and interests first. I treat people like people, not numbers on a chalkboard or in a spreadsheet cell. I create *client-centered* solutions and networks *aligned* with this philosophy. As a result, the client feels like they are being taken care of by a *dream team*.

> *"It isn't just about getting a positive return for the client or for me. It is about getting a positive return for the client's advisory network. There is no competition. The people who learn what I share, are elevated by looking after everyone's interest."*
>
> **–Mark W. Purnell**

Building a successful practice takes patience and knowhow. At times, you will experience great challenges. Many times, in my career, I had to learn things the hard way. But I was fortunate to have mentors; I was willing to listen to them, and they helped me do things more simply, and more effectively. Let my book and me be that mentor for you.

So, if you are:

- **Stressed** out trying to get everything done on a deadline, doing too much for too little return;

- **Confused** about how to reliably gain more clients, keep them, and make sure everyone is happy with their results;

- **Worried** about what your competition is doing, and how to differentiate yourself in an already fiercely competitive industry;

INTRODUCTION

- **Frustrated** because you know you must invest to build your practice but are strapped for cash, and
- **Feel unsupported** and don't know *who* you can trust...

If any of those describe you or your situation, don't worry.

That's normal. We have all been there, and you're not alone.

Fortunately, at least part-of your solution is right here in your hands.

In this book, you will learn how to:

- GAIN high-net-wealth clients without having to spend a fortune.
- Develop WINNING strategies for your clients that aren't based on "luck," and strategies that will thrill them time after time.
- Build and SUSTAIN your practice in the short term and for the long-run.
- Secure HIDDEN profit streams that are right under your nose.
- Be THE PREFERRED ADVISOR clients and other consultants in your community think of first whenever they have a want or need.
- Turn your competition and foes into raving FANS.
- BUILD and lead a winning team of advisors.
- Get MORE done in less time.

I have taken great effort to paint the landscape of the industry you are working in and simplify complicated concepts, so you can understand them, and apply them fast.

> "Mark, for over 40 years has been open to try new things and when his ideas have failed to work, he has an uncanny way of learning from his mistakes." ...Mark fails fast, learns quick and pivots swiftly. It is his refreshing direct and honest approach with people that I particularly appreciate."
>
> –Phillip Hurtt

> "You can learn a lot from an individual who has sold his practice three times."
>
> –Mill Harris

> "Don't beg... Negotiate... A Simple and ingenious approach..."
>
> –Ken Jubert

If you're at all curious about getting personalized help, I've opened up my calendar to give you a FREE private consultation.

Use this link to book your free call now.
MarkPurnell.net/bonus

–Mark W. Purnell, CIMA

SECTION I:
The Opportunity You Have

CHAPTER 1

Your Big Opportunity In A Fiercely Competitive Market

*"Don't wish your life was good,
Don't hope it will get better
Get up and make it amazing!"*
– Unknown

ARE YOU READY TO get some new clients and grow your business? Of course you are!

But FIRST, you will need to understand a few trends.

In this chapter, I cover a few *key industry trends* you may or may not be familiar with. I'll also share what I think you can do *with* those trends, what remains *unchanged*, and

CH 1 - YOUR BIG OPPORTUNITY

how you can position yourself to succeed in the immediate future, and for the long-term.

This chapter sets the scene for a lot of what we will discuss in later chapters, and the foundational basis you learn here will move you forward to the day when you *will* onboard your dream clients!

You will learn how to benefit from:

1. The emergence of a counterculture that suggests investors are not sold on robotic automation as much as they prefer customization.
2. The huge opportunity that is provided for the advisor, and their team, during a "moment of truth experience" to demonstrate **character, courage, skill** and the desire to embrace the **client's vision** of success.
3. The transfer of wealth from the baby boomers to their children.
4. Aging of established advisors, many of whom are approaching retirement age.
5. Understanding the interests of women and their role as the **"Family Steward."**
6. A changing financial landscape and the *"one thing that won't change!"*

It's great to be enthusiastic and ready to act, but you don't want to jump into a river that's flowing downstream and begin swimming upstream. You will get burned out working too hard to cover very little distance.

The solution? It's much less taxing to swim *with* the current. Now, that's easier said than done. Because first, you must know where the current is heading and what the currents are doing.

Once you understand what the current is doing, you can position yourself in the right place, at the right time, and do the right things.

The result? You can get where you want to go faster and easier and you can *respond* more effectively to unexpected changes.

So, keep an eye open for the opportunities that lie ahead that can help you grow your business while systematizing your practice so that when you are ready to retire you can realize its maximum value.

CH 1 - YOUR BIG OPPORTUNITY

1 - Make Friends with Trends

What changes and trends should you be aware of? The industry is experiencing four main changes[1]. With these changes, come big questions for advisors:

1. **Technology:** "Am I going to be replaced by robots?"
2. **Fees**: "Are fees going to be so scarce that I can no longer run a profitable practice?"
3. **Transparency:** "Is increased transparency good or bad for my business?"
4. **Talent and Succession:** "What's my opportunity here?"

Technology

- "Are robots destined to become sophisticated and reliable enough to replace my advisor?"
- "Is your advice worth paying for?"
- "Why can't I just be my own advisor?"

High-net-worth and wealthy families are <u>not interested</u> in robo-solutions. The financial needs of these families

---

[1] "10 disruptive trends in wealth management | Deloitte US | Financial Services Consulting." Deloitte United States. February 02, 2017. Accessed February 04, 2018. https://www2.deloitte.com/us/en/pages/consulting/articles/ten-disruptive-trends-in-wealth-management.html.

change over time and they are interested in having *an active and ongoing relationship* with a financial advisor.

Furthermore, what I find interesting is that since 2015, a counterculture to the robot-movement has begun to emerge. The leading theory is that investors are not sold on automation as much as they prefer *customization*.

Clients and firms are not ready to abandon the personal touch of a traditional client experience during a "moment of truth" experience.

A "moment of truth" is defined as an instance of contact or interaction between a client and a firm (through a product, sales force, or visit) that gives the client an opportunity to form or change an impression about the firm. This is good news for the financial advisor. Moments of truth often occur when the client has a problem and the opportunity to create a deeper emotional bond is greater when raised emotions exist. Escalated emotions demand a high-performance response from the advisor. Don't make the mistake of overinvesting in humdrum transactions but differentiate your team through the client experiences that matter. Delivery of investment advice and past performance or fee inquiries are critical interactions. This is where customization thrills the client.

Fees & Transparency

The Deloitte report on disruptive trends in wealth management notes:

CH 1 - YOUR BIG OPPORTUNITY

> *"The decline in the average percentage of assets for new accounts opened in the last 12 months dropped to 1.07% in 2016, from 1.12% in 2015 according to a survey by Price Metrix. After a decline from 1.13% in 2014, to 1.15% in 2013, the average asset-based fee was 1.13% in 2016.*

Advisor fees have become *increasingly compressed* for financial advisors.

Now, thanks to new fiduciary rules proposed by the Department of Labor regarding advice on retirement accounts, advisors will be required to disclose all fees charged and the total amount of these fees, to clients.

The Internet has also provided an online platform for both clients and advisors, increasing the *transparency* of advisor fees. Especially amongst millennial and Generation X clients who are used to shopping for products and services online.

The question is: Will the transparency of the proposed fiduciary rules and advisor fees help bring down the cost of financial advice? You would think so. But it is hard to say.

Why? Because I'm not sure that all clients could understand how their financial advisors are compensated even if you explained it to them. This has been my experience with the industry for 30+ years.

The financial services industry, and especially advisors compensated via commissions, do little to add transparency to the conversation as it pertains to the cost of advice.

Additionally, I suspect these disclosures will be written in terms that are not intuitive to many clients reading them.

What does this mean for us advisors? The trusted advisor has a real opportunity to serve the investing public and help them understand the cost and value of advice.

What's certain is, as clients become more knowledgeable, informed, and sophisticated, they will continue to seek out even better arrangements that maximize their benefit and lower their risk. *This is what advisors ought to do for their clients anyway.*

As you seek to acquire and retain more clients in the future, you will increasingly have to find ways to *add value* or *communicate value* that meet your client's fundamental values and wants.

You will have to understand their deeper *drivers* for what's truly important to their lives, and the lives of their stakeholders (family, friends, colleagues, networks, causes, etc.). You will come to understand more and more of these considerations as you read each chapter in this book.

Talent and Succession

The next big change I want to cover, is what I call the *changing of the financial advisor guard.* Based on a 2015 Deloitte research "10 Disruptive Trends in Wealth Management" and confirmed by my personal observations over the last 30+ years; two major demographic shifts will impact financial advisors in the coming decade:

1. **The aging of established advisors, many of whom are approaching retirement age.**

   The advisor population is aging rapidly and preparing for a significant transition. With 43% of US financial advisors over the age of 55 years old, the industry is contending with the expectation that approximately one-third of this current workforce will retire in the next 10 years.

2. **The transfer of wealth from the baby boomers to their children.**

   The baby boomers represent the largest fee pool for financial services firms. Almost one in every five baby boomers already have investable assets of more than $500,000.

Both trends could result in a massive dislocation of existing advisor/client relationships. In other words, *assets will likely change both owners and advisors.*

What are the challenges posed by these trends? And what do they mean for you? Succession planning is the first challenge. Many sole advisors are reaching generally accepted retirement ages and will need to partner and merge to accomplish common goals.

In the absence of *adequate succession planning*, it seems likely that many financial practitioners will find it more difficult to make the transition exactly as intended. This is one reason the consolidation and merger and acquisition of financial advisory practices are likely to become even more important.

Later, in the book, we will examine using coaches and consultants when establishing processes, systems, and delegated responsibilities that enable an advisor to create an optimal succession and exit strategy.

Next, the industry will need to recruit and train nearly 240,000 advisors just to maintain current service levels. But talent is not an issue for the advisory community. Competitive compensation and exciting career options guarantee a steady stream of capable, diverse, and under-represented individuals who will be drawn to the industry.

What I have seen is a severe lack of training among even some of the most prominent firms. In addition to essential skills coaching and engaging prospects; clients today require a strong personal brand, consistent with corporate standards and messaging.

In many cases, firms need to develop fresh approaches utilizing new methods, and doing so will require a substantial and "real" commitment of resources.

That is a catch-22. Many advisors who are well trained, often leave to join other competing broker dealers. As an advisor, this gives you great bargaining power. Those who want to build a practice and hire other advisors will have to think of ways to build trust, loyalty, and something "extra" to retain key team players.

Fortunately for you, you have access to this book. Let it be your mentor. Even if someone isn't willing to commit resources to your training, you have committed to your *own* learning and development.

CH 1 - YOUR BIG OPPORTUNITY

Let's continue the discussion about the changing of the guards. As the growing generational gap between advisors and investors occurs, you can expect some weakened client-advisor relationships.

- *For the older advisor serving the younger investor:* The older advisors who have been slow to adopt new tools and mobile channels, will find it hard to understand the *specific needs and preferences* of a younger generation of wealth.

- *For the younger advisor serving the older investor:* The younger advisor will have to adjust to the fact that the older investor may not be well-versed in modern tools and mobile channels, and again, will find it hard to understand the *specific needs and preferences* of the older generation of wealth.

What do all these trends tell you? Amidst the trends are opportunities to gain, and equally, opportunities to lose.

Knowing the trends is what empowers you to make a choice.

The common denominator is you, the entrepreneurial-minded advisor. How you position yourself, what actions you take, and how you respond to a fiercely competitive, exciting, and rewarding industry will forecast the level of your success.

II - Where is the Money Flowing and Where is It Going?

While it is true that most of the wealth in the world is held by the baby boomer generation, I don't recommend putting all your eggs in one basket. That's a matter of preference. But in my experience, no wise investor puts all their money in one stock. They pick a combination. I believe the same approach is useful when you consider *who* you want to focus on serving in the industry. So, if you have baby boomer clientele, a possible strategy would be to take a family approach and focus on serving the entire family unit including the parents and children. You will become the family advisor who captures intergenerational wealth transfers as they occur. Doing so has obvious implications for your team-building efforts as well as you and your team will meet the client needs of a diverse age demographic that is geographically dispersed.

I have embraced the perspective of Wendy Connett, who has been a financial journalist and thought leader for more than 20 years. In her analysis "How Financial Advisors Can Capture the $240B Worth of Fees Coming by 2030"[2], Connett summarized the following regarding the growth opportunity in the wealth management industry:

> *"Household assets are expected to grow by 60% over the next 15 years, increasing to more than $140 trillion by 2030 and*

---

[2] Connett, Wendy. "How Financial Advisors Can Capture the $240B Worth of Fees Coming by 2030" Investopedia. February 5, 2016. Accessed January 8, 2018.

CH 1 - YOUR BIG OPPORTUNITY

> *generating as much as $240 billion in wealth management fees for the taking, according to research from the Deloitte Center for Financial Services.*
>
> *"The report cautions that wealth managers looking to capture such wealth should not court up and coming millennials at the expense of any baby boomer and Generation X clients. The Deloitte report forecasts how generational wealth will evolve across four generations: The Silent Generation (folks born between 1925 and 1942), baby boomers, Generation X and millennials through 2030. It also highlights what wealth managers should consider when it comes to adjusting business models to adapt and cater to the changing demographics of wealth in the next 15 years.*
>
> *"'Wealth management in the United States is a huge business today and it is about to get even bigger,' said Gauthier Vincent, a principal with Deloitte Consulting LLP and leader of Deloitte's wealth management practice, in a statement. 'But this market is likely to become increasingly segmented by unique generational needs.'*

How the Generations Stack Up

Baby boomers will continue to be the wealthiest generation in the U.S. through 2030. They will also remain the largest fee pool for financial services firms. They will have more than $53 trillion in wealth in 2030 representing about 45% of total household wealth.

Connett also asserts:

> "Almost one in five baby boomers already have investable assets of more than $500,000.
>
> "This generation's share of net household wealth will peak at 50% by 2020. It will slip to less than 45% by 2030, after which it will quickly taper off as mortality rates rise.
>
> "As for Generation X, it will have the highest increase in share of national wealth through 2030. This generation will grow from under 14% of total net wealth in 2015 to almost 31% by 2030."

The report maintains financial services firms that have not yet woken up to Generation X's potential may be too late to the party. About 37% of Gen X had more than $100,000 in investable assets as of 2015.

> "While the wealth of millennial individuals will grow the fastest, they will only account for less than 20% of national household wealth in 2030. Most are unlikely to become consumers of top-tier wealth services anytime soon.
>
> "'All that said, I don't recommend taking your eye off the ball on this new generation of investors, as Gen X and millennials will make up half of wealth in 2030,' said Vincent."

As they mature, millennials' financial assets are projected to grow from $1.4 trillion in 2015 to $11.3 trillion in 2030. Currently, only 14% of millennials have more than $100,000 in investable assets.

CH 1 - YOUR BIG OPPORTUNITY

The Silent Generation

The Silent Generation, whose youngest members are 70 years old, receive far less attention than it deserves, the report maintains. These folks represent nearly $24 trillion in wealth. While the wealth of this generation will begin to taper off soon, the report warns that ignoring them may be a mistake. It points out that the average American man who is age 70 today is likely to live for another 14 years and that a 70-year-old American woman will likely live for another 16 years.

> "Much of the wealth of the Silent Generation will be passed on to younger generations over the next two decades. This presents opportunities for advisors to build relationships with the heirs of this generation to create more stickiness in their customer base. While these heirs might not be the most profitable clients today, they might be once they come into their inheritance."

My conclusion? Mass marketing to affluent clients across all generations as a sole strategy is not as effective as it once was. Heirs who are not profitable clients today can become profitable clients when they come into their inheritance. This is why becoming an "intergenerational family advisor" may be a prudent consideration.

When they do, they will need help from advisors who can *realign their advice* to accommodate the values and interests of these new beneficiaries.

Advisors that plan to retire in less than 10 years may find some comfort focusing on and serving the young baby boomer and Silent Generation. By 2030 it's expected that these investors will still control 45% of US wealth and retiring advisors might find their "sunset" arrangements to be less attractive to younger advisors in light of the anticipated rise in mortality rates of this cohort.

But an advisor with a 10-year or more horizon will also want to maintain substantial focus on the Gen X and millennial demographic when assembling a multigenerational advisory team and constructing their succession/retirement plan. These generations are the ones likely to make up for at least half the wealth in 2030 and beyond.

III - Respect and Embrace the Values and Interests of Women

Women approach investments differently. Women tend to embrace a financial planning approach to making investment decisions, as opposed to men who will allow the investment strategy to drive the decision making.

I have learned that women like to engage me on "real life" problems, like the costs of long-term care for aging parents, during the planning process. By incorporating, these common concerns into the investment strategy conversation, women tend to be more confident and secure in their decisions.

Many women feel the focus on values and community is vital and lacking in the male-dominated world of finance. Taking the long view and evaluating the purpose of money is a healthy and reality-based way to relate to money and investing.

Adopting this perspective has enabled me to focus on what matters most in my life and serve others in a powerful way.

For years, I focused on how big the pile of money was. Focusing on values and priorities have shifted my thinking. I am now clearer about what those are and can steer the money to what matters most in life.

This new perspective has led to far more conscious choices, more satisfaction with money, greater appreciation for what I do have, less stress, and more happiness.

And if that's considered a more feminine perspective on money, I'll take that any day!

In Chapter 2, you will learn about my high-net-worth clients, Bob and Shirley Greenhouse. Shirley handled the business affairs and had learned a lot about investing from her mother. Not only was she concerned about embracing conservative investment principles, but she wanted to continue the family traditions of gifting during her lifetime, and observe her offspring managing and enjoying the benefits of their inheritance.

Bob and I handled the decisions surrounding investment strategy, portfolio management, and tax planning, but both Bob and I knew that Shirley's concerns and vision of success were equally important.

Women need to be dealt with on an individual basis, and many times in the financial services industry, it is thought to be a man's game. That is not the case.

We need to start listening to what women think and what they specifically need as individuals and for their families.

This doesn't mean that women are a more meaningful niche than men when it comes to a product or portfolio strategy.

The danger is that the financial advisor could overlook this huge opportunity, and not pay attention to the role that women have in the consumption of financial services.

Women have made incredible strides in the past 50 years, and the wealth and power they hold will only increase in years

CH 1 - YOUR BIG OPPORTUNITY

to come. This change has come as women have also moved to fill 52 percent of management, and professional and related positions in the country, according to Bank of Montreal's Wealth Institute[3]. Moving up the ranks has made women the primary breadwinners in 40 percent of U.S. households. Women-owned businesses now account for 30 percent of all privately-owned enterprises, employing 7.8 million Americans. Women are either making decisions directly about their 401k, and personal investments or they are influencing their spouse's decisions. In either event, paying attention to her needs and concerns is smart.

Women control about half the wealth in the United States, but according to the Bank of Montreal's Wealth Institute, they're expected to be in control of about $22 trillion of the wealth by 2020. Sadly, some in the wealth management industry might not be quite ready for 2020. A portion of the wealth management industry might argue that women control substantially more than two-thirds of US wealth *indirectly*.

My experience working with families suggests that women have a huge influence on the selection of financial advisors and the services that are valued and demanded by the high-net-worth consumer.

I offer that women will inherit assets from parents, siblings and unfortunately, sometimes, from their children.

---

3 Gorman, Ryan. "Women now control more than half of US personal wealth, which 'will only increase in years to come'." Business Insider. April 07, 2015. Accessed February 04, 2018. http://www.businessinsider.com/women-now-control-more-than-half-of-us-personal-wealth-2015-4.

This is in addition to the assets they are building and saving for themselves.

A key component of my practice over the last 30 years has focused on the ability to <u>communicate with clients in a way that embraced and respected the values and interests of women</u>. Specifically, I would call attention to a consumer characteristic I have coined the "Family Steward."

> *A Family Steward is the person in the family who looks out for other family members including spouses, children, parents, siblings, and grandchildren. - Mark Purnell*

The Family Steward, in my experience, is a person looking out for the financial interests of these individuals and can also extend beyond family and might include a co-worker, neighbor or friend. This overlooked center of influence is most often a woman, but it can be a man.

When there is a financial event[4] in this person's network, the Family Stewards are concerned about how the financial consequences of the event are going to be handled. The Family Steward is generally interested in financial literacy and connecting the family member with trusted advisors. They are a connector of people and resources within their extensive network.

---

[4] An event that catalyzes the need to make a financial decision. For example: divorce, death in a family, children going to college, relocating homes, setting up a new business, etc.

IV - The One Thing That Won't Change

In over 30 years, I've seen a lot of change in the delivery of financial advice; I have offered advice through unprecedented world events and extremely volatile financial markets.

From Black Monday to the stock market crash of 1987, the Asian financial crisis of 1997, the Dot-Com bubble of 2000, the events of September 11, 2001, all the way to the resulting market downturn through 2002, the financial crisis of 2007, and the subsequent great recession, each of these events have brought a great deal of uncertainty to advisors and their clients. These cumulative experiences have produced the remedies and actions required by investors to obtain the best results possible and will be the desired model going forward.

Over those same 30+ years, I've seen a lot of administrative and industry change also. In 1984, clients were given seven days to settle a trade and most of my clients would place an order and mail a check to cover the trade.

Consequently, I was asked to deliver the securities to the client for safekeeping instead of holding them in a custodian account. Commissions and fees were much higher for transactions and for the first six years of my career I did not have a "quote machine" at my desk to provide market prices that today are streamed to my watch and mobile phone.

Given the projected accelerated rate of change, I expect one thing will remain the same: The investing public and wealthy families will "want," they will not "need," a financial advisor to talk to about the issues they're facing concerning their financial affairs and their family's needs—both of which are intertwined.

Families will want someone who fully understands their issues and concerns and–who–provides client-centered solutions that evolve as their complex and unpredictable lives unfold.

CHAPTER 2

What High-Net-Worth Clients Really Want

"Clients want advisors to simplify the complicated and treat them as an individual."
—Barth Guilette

I - What High-Net-Worth Clients Really Want From Their Advisors

ABOUT 25 YEARS AGO, a wealthy couple, Bob and Shirley Greenhouse, with three children were positioned to inherit substantial assets from her family. The attorney involved offered the idea of disclaiming the assets to their children to avoid creating a taxable estate at their eventual deaths. Their concern was that the children had little experience handling investments.

<u>I shared the vision that I would:</u>

- Work with each of the children and advise and guide them using the same prudent family strategies that had been successfully employed;

- Coordinate joint meetings with the parents on occasion, as needed, or desired, so they could see the progress the children were making or not making, and

- Ensure the annual gifting program we were contemplating would contribute to the portfolios growing even faster.

The plan has worked just as we had envisioned, and we have had over 100 meetings over the last 25 years. The children have learned and experienced handling investments through all types of market conditions, under the observation and guidance of a now 90-year-old parent. We have started the process with the grandchildren.

High potential clients desire these "out of the box" or "avoid the herd" approaches to solve problems. This was all accomplished because I made the "client's vision" my vision. I helped realize multigenerational planning with their external team of professional advisors and expanded the avenue to promote the family tradition of investing, growing capital, and transitioning it to the next generation.

Top advisors can understand the client's vision and make it their own.

Now, I want to add that we all have "blind spots" and the high-net-worth client likes to be educated about new ideas/concepts and enjoy "AHA" moments that are not condescending but can be discovered through queries and conclusions reached collaboratively.

Subsequently, these clients will look to you as a sounding board regularly. You become someone who gives them a sense of clarity and peace of mind about questions they have, or questions people have of them. They might be CEOs, they might be high-profile entertainers or athletes. You can trust they're approached all the time about money topics.

One high-profile client in an East Coast city was constantly bombarded with investment proposals. Specifically, I recall one incident where a new adviser to the industry was trying to sell him on his new insurance program. I flew in to help my client out. We had dinner with the new adviser, and we showed the other adviser the client's financial plan.

Then, we demonstrated where and why the investment was not an appropriate fit for the client at that time. We had to do some due diligence on the proposal at first because although there were existing benefits, they just weren't the right benefits to fit into the client's situation.

That's an example of using a sounding board to air out an idea and work with a client's adviser. It brings a thrill

CH 2 - WHAT HIGH-NET-WORTH CLIENTS REALLY WANT

to the client to see you are working in their very best interest.

As you can imagine, doing all of the above involves quite some time, energy, and effort. But that's also *exactly* what high-net-worth individuals (HNWI)s and families want.

They want an advisor who is busy enough that they don't have time for prospecting new clients, and who spends 80-90% of their time working on existing client matters. If you aren't sincerely up for that, then the path of being the trusted advisor everyone raves about might not be for you. You do this for the love and for the service. It's about putting others' needs at the forefront.

Consider yourself a financial tour guide. When I take a trip to New York City, I would like my guide to tell me what is coming next. I like them to anticipate and help me to anticipate the attractions. If I were going to the Statue of Liberty, I would love to hear the tour guide make this statement in advance:

> *"As we approach the Statue of Liberty it's going to be on your right side and available to view for only 30 seconds out your window. If you want to take a picture you should move to that side of the bus and have your camera ready. We're going to arrive in five minutes, so think about what you want to do and be prepared to act accordingly."*

When I say: "tour guide," I mean your client is looking for someone who can stay abreast of changing market conditions and laws that apply to them as a high-net-worth individual. They want to know how those two components will impact their lives. They don't like surprises.

Therefore, high-net-worth clients look for *evidence* that the advisor can anticipate their needs often—before they'll realize they need it for themselves.

When a 40-year-old, single, self-employed physician inherited $600,000 in assets from her mother, I immediately scheduled a meeting with the Certified Public Account (CPA). That way, we could develop a strategy around how estimated taxes would need to be monitored during the year.

Having a second variable income stream of dividends, capital gains, and municipal bond income could impact the CPA's method of calculating the estimated income tax payments. Without taking these planning steps, the client could potentially be unhappy with their year-end tax picture and be upset with me, the CPA or both of us.

Your desire is to know their biggest concern. This is often stated as a question, such as, *"How will these assets be passed on to the next generation?"* That was the biggest concern my elderly clients had in the example I gave earlier.

Then you do for your clients what they can't do for themselves. In my example, I helped educate their children to a level where their parents would be satisfied their children could handle their investments after they were gone.

Here are a few questions you must have *clear* answers for:

- **What can you do for your clients that they can't do for themselves?** High-net-worth individuals and families want you to do what they can't do for themselves. It sounds very generic. But that is the key. High-net-worth individuals and families have a unique set of values, for themselves, each other, and in most cases, for the wider community.

Understanding what their priorities are and communicating how you can help them achieve those priorities in ways they can't accomplish themselves, will lead to great opportunities for you and your practice.

- **Do you understand your value proposition and what the Alpha is you are offering in the investment world?**

We talk about Alpha being the value received from an investment return that is above and beyond the return to the market. It's the value the manager brings because they have either selected good stocks or they have made a good asset allocation decision.

In the advisory world, the Alpha typically represents the premium services an advisor offers to their clients and that value proposition needs to be very well communicated for the most part.

Here's what this all boils down to.

Clients want something I call: **Client-Centered and Coordinated Strategies.**

Clients want the basic components in terms of *service descriptions* such as an investment plan, an asset allocation strategy, risk management and disaster planning, global diversification, etc.

However, what they really want, is to have all their affairs and interests *coordinated*. They want to know the gears in their machine mesh and work together, that they have a team of aligned advisors who are advocating for the ongoing realization of their highest aspirations.

Let's look at an example of what a client typically does when they hire investment advisors to diversify their investments. Typically, the client asks about the advisor's investment specialty. To diversify and attempt to reduce risk they will employ several advisors, at different firms.

These other advisors do not communicate with each other and they execute a strategy that is more "advisor-centered" because it's the advisor's preferred strategy, not the client's preferred strategy.

The potential risk is that the client's goal of diversification is never accomplished because the client has selected advisors that are appealing and familiar and are often <u>duplicative</u> and not complementary. Therefore, increasing the risk of the overall portfolio. Put simply, they aren't *coordinated with one* another.

Prior to the financial crisis of 2008, the financial sector had been viewed as a conservative fundamental holding in a portfolio and during the resulting market decline, it became evident the sector was held in many portfolios that were not coordinated, thus creating an undesired and unintended overweight position.

Let me give you a simpler example. A client does not want to coordinate insurance coverage of their investment property with the family's lake cottage.

CH 2 - WHAT HIGH-NET-WORTH CLIENTS REALLY WANT

Or when they pursue an aggressive investment and growth strategy, they don't want to coordinate what the tax implications are and learn in what ways it impacts their overall goals and dreams.

They would expect *you*, their advisor, to:

1. Ask for a call/meeting with their CPA to plan for taxes.

2. Prepare for your annual meetings by putting it on the calendar and asking for statements so that you can update their investment plan, distribution plan, and growth plan.

3. Schedule the planning meeting.

That's what they want you to do. Clients love to see their advisers collaborating and making sure that strategies are being implemented across their portfolio. It is one of the biggest ways we can generate trust and thrill our clients.

How do you get people aligned to do this, especially when there can only be so many advisors involved in managing your clients' wealth and affairs? That's a topic we will cover in a later chapter.

For now, understand the extent you can ensure their affairs are coordinated, is the extent you are perceived to be of *value* to the family. They cannot afford a family office, but as a top advisor, you become their "virtual family office."

Here's a strategy I recently used to prep for a client's third quarter review meetings/conversations.

A TRUSTED FINANCIAL ADVISOR

<u>I analyzed their portfolio and determined the following:</u>

- $1.6 million managed account is up 11% or ~$150,000 YTD.
- $320,000 of unrealized gains.
- $151,000 realized in current year.
- $121,000 realized in prior year.

I will call the client to review their capital gains in the current year and ask them the following: Are they below or above the expectations the CPA used in their federal tax estimate calculations?

Because I don't want them to be uninformed and surprised about their tax bill, I would review the following options.

<u>I'd review this with both their investment manager and CPA:</u>

- Are there losses that can be taken to offset the $151,000 already realized?
- Should the manager be asked to "freeze" any further gains?
- Are there appreciated stocks that should be donated to a charitable entity?
- 9/15 tax payments were just made; should the next January tax estimate be increased to avoid penalties? Because the investment income is $30,000 higher than the CPA estimated.

CH 2 - WHAT HIGH-NET-WORTH CLIENTS REALLY WANT

I'm *anticipating* the client's needs before they even identify they have them. Coordinated advice is proactive and better serves your client than being reactionary.

Coordinating the strategy requires being the client advocate and communicating with other advisors either directly or indirectly (through the client) so implementation is accomplished throughout the client's assets.

The client gets an intuitive feeling that the advisory team is using a repeatable "process" for delivering consistent coordinated outcomes that started with a complete financial diagnosis and will result in the best possible outcomes.

In doing the above, you will have demonstrated the following to the client and the other members of their advisory team:

- **You are a co-owner in their vision for success.** That means you build loyal bonds of trust *akin* to positioning you as "part of the family." This increases your client retention rates.

- **You are an advisor they can confidently refer to other people and families in their networks.** Subsequently, you gain more clients without spending a fortune. You also eliminate the competition.

- **You get *more done* in less time.** We will speak more about this later as we cover strategies to make you the *preferred go-to* person anytime a client has a query. Subsequently, this positions you as the *Gatekeeper* for all your clients' affairs.

- **You make their lives easier.** Upon seeing your elevated professionalism, the client's other advisors will also become your advocates and marketing partners. This becomes valuable when you need a second set of eyes or a complimentary review for a special client or prospect. This is the power of advocacy.

In the coming chapters, I will be sharing more insights and distinctions into how you can achieve client-centered and coordinated strategies. But for now, I'll repeat something that can never be repeated enough if you are to become the trusted advisor everyone raves about:

High-net-worth individuals and families want the "things" you can do for them that they can't do for themselves. Period.

Let me stop here and provide a couple of examples of what I mean by "things."

1. Using your professional connections to provide a complimentary review of a client's potential transaction.

2. Using your knowledge of a client's investment portfolio to highlight possible implications on tax, legal or banking matters with their other advisors. Clients are thrilled with this type of interaction.

II- Why Most Advisors Fail at Achieving Client-Centered and Coordinated Strategies

While a large percentage of professionals profess their intent to be client-centered, many of them are not effectively working in this manner.

Why? First, it's risky! When the deal is done, will the people you worked with and negotiated against say you and your clients conducted yourselves professionally and with integrity? You must be prepared to work outside your area of competency. You may have to learn alongside your client, and that may feel uncertain.

Secondly, it takes more brain-work. Each client is like a snowflake and requires a customized approach. Being client-centered is more than adopting a mental attitude and ethical stance. It is also a skill set.

To be client-centered, professionals must effectively understand their clients. Failing to profile them effectively restricts your ability to provide viable, professional, and worthwhile solutions.

Lastly, it requires that you manage how you are perceived by clients and their prospects. I asked Frank Campanale, (a 40+-year industry innovator and thought leader), "Why do most advisors never achieve client-centered and coordinated strategies?"

He said, "The advisor's time is limited, regulations, and firm policies are many, and the financial landscape is complex."

Many advisors make recommendations too soon without using a "holistic" client-centric process (sometimes ignoring illiquid assets and credit/debt issues) and they don't recognize there is a direct connection between the professionalism of their support staff, and how they personally are viewed by their clients and prospects. *Most advisors don't understand their support staff is the public face of their practice.*

At this stage, you might be feeling overwhelmed or unsure if you can pull this off. I did, too, back in the day. But that's why you are reading this book, because you know it takes some learning.

You know that getting help from others who have done what you want to do, is a great way to *shorten* your learning curve. And you know there is *less competition* when you aim higher because not many advisors will be *willing* to do what I share with you in this book.

The benefits of achieving these goals are very rewarding. In the following chapters, I'll reveal more detail and insight about how you can create client-centered and co-ordinated strategies.

CHAPTER 3

The Formula For A Profitable Practice

"The E-Myth ("Entrepreneurial Myth") is the mistaken belief that most businesses are started by people with tangible business skills, when in fact, most are started by 'technicians' who know nothing about running a business."
– Michael E. Gerber

PAY ATTENTION TO WHAT I share in this chapter, and it could shed years off your growth curve.
In 1989, I sold my independent financial advisory practice to the full-service regional brokerage firm, Blunt Ellis & Loewi, a division of Kemper, and I became a W-2 employee.

From 1989 to 2007, I operated under the Kemper Securities, (CAPMARC Securities for a few days) EVEREN

CH 3 - THE FORMULA FOR A PROFITABLE PRACTICE

Securities, First Union Securities, and Wachovia Securities. That's six firms over 18 years, and I never changed my address.

From 2008 until 2016, I operated in a practice with a partner as an independent under the Wells Fargo Advisors FINET channel where I served as the branch manager.

What I learned from clients over this time frame was that even though I was an employee of the various firms, I was the "brand" because they did business with me. Their view, which became my view, was that I was a "franchise owner-operator." It didn't matter whose name was on the statement and the custodian of their assets. If my service team was in place, they were good.

It became very clear that "moments of truth" incidents (and there were many) were my ultimate responsibility to fix and make good for the client. I needed to accept my calling as an innovator and express my entrepreneurial spirit by keenly providing unique insight and guidance through the tumultuous times of the:

- Asian financial crisis 1997

- Dot-Com Bubble of 1999

- September 11 Attack and Market Downturn 2001-2002, and the

- Financial Crisis of 2007 and the resulting Great Recession.

The firm was very supportive of a million-dollar producer (attained in 1999), but I needed to examine my profit formula. The pertinent questions included; how was I going to fund and accomplish a balance of interests that included my clients, my family, my community, and my philanthropic interests?

Most advisors see themselves as employees of a firm, meaning:

(Gross production of advisor/team * payout from firm) = the Financial Advisor's (FA's) compensation

They know or assume that all costs associated with serving the client are to be borne by the firm and therefore, the advisor is not in control of serving their client.

This formula is designed to build loyalty and trust with the firm and is "advisor-centric" whereas the firm's marketing view is to brand to the firm. For example, the firm doesn't care if you attend a client's funeral; it's not in the job description. The firm might give you a travel and expense budget for serving the client.

But what if your budget to deliver your personalized client service model exceeds your firm allotment? <u>Budgeting from the FA's compensation will provide the funding</u>.

It's one thing to make a lot of money for the firm where you are employed. But as an advisor, the money you make for the firm isn't always going to help you make the money you want to take home. Especially if you want to deliver customized client-centered and coordinated solutions that will thrill your clientele.

CH 3 - THE FORMULA FOR A PROFITABLE PRACTICE

You are constantly forced to think about other costs/investments you must make to build and sustain your practice (marketing), and the money that comes to you (your profit), sufficiently supports *your* personal interests, too.

In the previous chapter, we touched on the importance of being client-centered and coordinated and taking care of your *clients'* business. This chapter focuses on taking care of *your* business. Both are necessary.

1 – What Does Your Profit Formula Look Like?

When I started my practice, I lived off a very *lean income*. Just enough to cover the basic costs. Any excess profit I made in my practice could be *reinvested* in business development activity to grow my practice.

A common mistake that financial advisors make is to think their payout from the firm all goes into their bank account. But when you are building your practice, you must realize there are *investments* you have to make in your practice in the short-term to benefit you in the long-term.

So, how do you determine your basic living costs? This is a very personal decision, but I would encourage advisors to live 30-40% below their income level.

Why? In 2001 and in 2008, because my clients were billed on asset-based fees, my compensation fell by 30% because gross production dropped to 30% due to client assets diminishing by that percentage.

Let's revisit the profit formula to incorporate your business development budget. The profit formula is expressed as:

(Gross production of advisor/team *payout from firm) -
(the Business Development Budget) =
Owner/lead advisor compensation (what's left)

CH 3 - THE FORMULA FOR A PROFITABLE PRACTICE

The Business Development Budget is expressed as expenses other than owner/lead advisor compensation such as:

- Payroll for additional staff
- Charitable gifting to support client philanthropy
- Meals
- Travel & Entertainment
- Professional Development
- Technology expenses

You want to be certain that what's left exceeds your *basic living costs*. As you can imagine, the more your compensation exceeds your basic living costs, the more money you have to invest in business development.

For example, today, my net payout from a 100% gross production is about 75%. But I only take home 18% as part of my compensation. That means I invest 57% of my gross production into business development.

But how do you determine how much of the business development budget you should set aside for each component? There's no perfect ratio. It's *your* profit formula. What works for you won't necessarily work for me.

Determining your profit formula is more art than science. But in the coming sections of this chapter, I'm going to share a few things you need to think about when it comes to working out your profit formula. And remember, what's effective one year might not be the next year. It's a growing and evolving plan.

II - The Seven "T's"

I look at seven T's when building a practice. These are as follows:

1. Time
2. Tools
3. Technology
4. Techniques
5. Team
6. Touch
7. Tithing

Time

You can't do everything yourself in your business. At the start, that may be the case. But you probably can't handle more than $30 million in AUM. Or between 30-60 households.

I had to figure out how to work fewer hours because I couldn't put it any more hours. I tried to meaningfully examine how I could be more productive and how I could get more out of the time I was already putting in.

The concept of doing the same business and working half the time began to resonate with me very deeply.

CH 3 - THE FORMULA FOR A PROFITABLE PRACTICE

Additionally (and this is something we will cover in more detail shortly), I knew I had to focus on doing what I do best, enjoy, and then hire the rest.

> *"Do what you enjoy.... then find others to employ."*
> **–Mark Purnell**

I had to gain clarity around the concept of an "individual performer" vs. an individual performer who functions as a member of a team.

Most FAs are individual performers, and a delicate balance must be struck when you either join a team or build a team. This can be a huge minefield, and I would highly encourage engaging a coach/mentor to help with a good design around training, incentives, investments, expenses, and compensation.

Sole advisors get to control what work tasks they take on and "my profit formula" vs. the "team's formula" is affected differently based on the outsourcing or delegation decisions.

The bottom line in "my profit formula" can be changed drastically by a decision to outsource functions or hiring a staff person to do the necessary tasks the advisor doesn't enjoy or wish to do anymore. It's an empowering and pivotal clarification when you reach this point in your business.

Money is time. Money can save you time. But how are you putting that time to its most productive use? If an advisor can generate $1,000 per hour in front of a qualified client and prospects, then buying a business development manager at $25 or $50 per hour is a very powerful decision. *It's called time leverage.*

Tools

You need to invest in new investment tools if you are going to customize pretty much every client solution.

Specifically, **a portfolio manager** will need a tool for investing assets, implementing investment strategy, and managing day-to-day portfolio trading.

A relationship manager will need a tool to summarize, maintain, and present client goals and progress toward achievement.

A business development manager needs a tool to maintain a "drip system" for marketing to existing clients, and new market clients that may be identified for future top 20 clients, and/or centers of influence. These tools may involve some technology components (see list below) or could be maintained manually.

I had to identify whether I was going to be a portfolio manager, a relationship manager or business development manager. I began to look at the investment toolbox to make sure it was as efficient as possible. Also, I did not require using some investment solutions or tools.

Technology

You need to embrace all the current and developing technologies for tasks that consume a lot of time. To find the most applicable innovations, you must demonstrate to your team that you are "open" to being on the cutting edge and will consider what is available. The technology you opt to use does have to be feasible for your budget since it will have an impact on your profit formula.

Claire Aiken, author of the book *The LinkedIn Guide for Financial Advisors*, offers these smart ideas. She covers several essential tech tools for financial advisors, including:

- Secure password storage
- A good CRM
- Financial planning software
- DOL Fiduciary Rule Compliance tools
- An online calendar scheduler
- Google Analytics

Do your research. While it is true that you are doing for your clients what they can't do for themselves, you can find technology tools to help you do what you *don't* want to do for yourself or *can't* do well yourself. Often, these tools are a lot more cost-effective than hiring a new full-time position.

Technique

The slowest way to learn anything is to take a "do it myself" approach. I personally hire many coaches and mentors (even today), so someone can help me look in my "blind spots."

For example, becoming a million-dollar producer is very different than becoming a $500,000 producer. In my case, I was continuing to think and act like a $500,000 producer, and I felt that approach was sufficient to lead me toward becoming a million-dollar producer.

Think about it, growing an orchard is far different than growing a rose even if both involve some sort of gardening. I had to become a better advisor, become immersed in my clients' issues, and share their visions of progress toward their goals and want what they wanted. Otherwise, I wouldn't get anywhere.

> **! BONUS TIP:**
>
> *Never leave a client exchange without repeating what you learned from them and what you are going to do with the information. Then deliver. Through listening intently, I could become more of an advocate. I had to embrace the advocacy position and the advocacy efforts for my clients and for their advisers, as well as for everybody else around me, including my teammates.*

CH 3 - THE FORMULA FOR A PROFITABLE PRACTICE

Team

Here's the problem: you're an investment professional, not a service professional. You didn't come into the industry to execute a service. You don't get compensated directly for it. Nor are you likely to have the time to personally deliver fast, friendly, and meticulous service.

The solution then is obvious: You must have a team. Furthermore, at least one member of your team should be a dedicated team member who answers the phones, manages the calendar, handles paperwork, and fulfills client requests. You need a team member who can return phone calls and emails in a timely manner.

Your practice must incorporate: a few other key roles as well:

1. **Business development manager.** A business development manager works to improve an organization's market position and achieve financial growth.

2. **Relationship manager.** A relationship manager is a professional who works to improve a firm's relationships with both partner firms and customers. I spend most of my time in this role. I advocate for all my staff, partner advisors, clients, and the important people in their lives. The service assistant also sits with this team.

3. **Portfolio manager.** A portfolio manager is a person or group of people responsible for investing assets, implementing investment strategies, and managing day-to-day portfolio trading.

In the beginning, your team might be "Me, Myself, and I." That's okay. That is often the case for advisors starting out. Just know you won't be able to handle more than $30 million in AUM. Or between 30-60 households.

You need a few key people on your team. And at one stage, you are going to have to decide where you want to focus most of your time. Remember, either do what you do best and hire the rest or do what you enjoy and find others to employ.

The key thing to note about "Team" is to learn to be an *advocate* for whoever is involved. There's always a way for everyone to win. Your role is to see it that way.

In my earlier days as an advisor, I had to learn to *stop selling* and start being an *advocate* for all the people I was trying to help. Decades later, this simple principle in action has been richly rewarding.

Here is a more detailed breakdown of my compensation once I account for key staff:

Gross Production	100%
Net Payout	75%
Salaries:	
Portfolio Manager	10%
Relationship Manager	10%
Business Development Manager	10%
Business Development Budget	10%
Client Marketing Budget	10%
Fixed Overhead	7%
Owner/Lead Advisor Compensation (what's left)	18%

CH 3 - THE FORMULA FOR A PROFITABLE PRACTICE

At the end of the chapter, you are going to work out a similar profit formula that works for you. Over time you are going to adjust and refine it.

Touch

Customization means keeping track of the *different touches* each client needs. You must figure out what will be the most effective for *their* style. To give you an example, does a client desire:

- A one-page report?
- A 20-page report?
- Both?

You must find out the answer. Today, a high-level summary meets the demand for some clients, while others want all the details. Still, other clients will desire both. With regards to modes of communication:

- Should I call, if so...home, cell, work? What time zone are they in?
- Email, text?
- Snail mail?

Now you might be thinking I am adding too much work to your plate. But remember, I have been doing this for 30+ years. I have been painting the landscape of what is involved to become the advisor everyone raves about.

When I started in the advising business, I didn't know all of what I am sharing with you. I put various elements into practice one bit at a time. I hired coaches and mentors to help me, too. As the old saying goes, *"How do you eat an elephant? One bite at a time."*

Earlier in the book, I mentioned why most advisors never achieve client-centered and coordinated strategies. Because it isn't an easy business to begin with. But that's where your opportunity lies. The big benefit of looking to achieve what most people don't achieve is: there's very little (or no) competition at the top.

Tithing

A tithe is a tenth part of a whole paid as a voluntary contribution or as a tax especially for the support of religious establishments. In my opinion, tithing applies to more than supporting religious establishments because there are many 501c3 entities with missions to improve and empower communities. *Tithing is a form of advocacy.* My mother called it "Putting your money where your mouth is."

When you practice tithing, your status in the community will be elevated. The main communication you give to others is: I am a resource for my community, and I am here to be of service.

Just imagine meeting someone like that. What's your experience with them? For most, it is one of trust and ad-

CH 3 - THE FORMULA FOR A PROFITABLE PRACTICE

miration. And *trust* is what you need if you want to do business with anybody.

I've embraced the idea of giving back to my community and taking a tenth of net income expressed as "**owner/lead advisor compensation.**" Additionally, a tenth would be allocated for the savings of the advisor.

You, too, can develop a budget to support community, religious, and philanthropic efforts. You will want to continue annually budgeting tithing as a part of your profit formula so that you can give back to the community.

Your clients and community at-large will recognize your sincerity, generosity, and passion for making a difference in a world that so desperately needs these efforts, leadership, and knowledge that a financial advisor represents. This all comes back to you, of course. It reflects on your practice, and enhances its reputation, strengthening your brand advocacy.

In a later chapter, I share more detailed strategies about how you can align your philanthropic interests and strengthen your reputation in the industry, using Donor Advised Funds (DAFs) and 990 Filings. Because you're supporting the community, it *does*, in fact, lead to the community supporting your practice.

III - Your Homework: Write Down Your Profit Formula

As you may have noticed, the 7 T's really have nothing to do with investments. Investments are a way to realize your intentions. The 7 T's pertain to your behavior and attitude toward serving your clients.

You get a profitable practice by helping others, mostly clients, and you can do for them what they can't do for themselves. This impact extends to enrich your life, and the lives in the community.

With the 7 T's in mind, work out a draft profit formula for yourself.

Think about how you would like to allocate the funds to the different T's.

For example, you have already invested time and some money into this book. Reading it should be part of your Business Development Budget.

Remember to factor in your payout that needs to match or exceed your basic living cost. This is a personal preference. Work out your initial profit formula:

**(Gross production of advisor/team * payout from firm) -
<u>(the Business Development Budget)</u>
=
Owner/lead advisor compensation (what's left)**

CH 3 - THE FORMULA FOR A PROFITABLE PRACTICE

One way to do this is to consider what investing in the different T's will effectively mean to your profit formula. How do you expect investing in the different T's will help you *increase* gross production, so your compensation (what's left) will increase over time?

I'll give you an example; you could invest 6% of gross production and allocate it as follows:

- 2% Coach and Mentor to examine and help you harvest your "blind spots" (Technique)
- 2% Technology for you and/or your teammates (Technology)
- 2% Donor Advised Funds (Tithing)

You don't have to do it the way I did. I'm not going to tell you how to run your business, but I can share some of my insights I've learned over the years. That's why I wrote this book.

SECTION II:
Maximize Gain & Minimize Pain

CHAPTER 4:

Get Known Without Spending A Fortune

"The beauty of life does not depend on how happy you are, but on how happy others can be because of you."
– Unknown

YOUR BRAND IS A big deal. As I discussed in an earlier chapter, it didn't matter what firm I was working with. If I was with my loyal clients, if it was my brand serving them, and the team that came with my brand, the client was good.

Your brand is an expression of your vision, values, and philosophy for life. "How you are perceived," as Frank Campanale said, "determines a lot about how clients decide whether to hire you or not." It also determines how other advisors position and spread your reputation. *That's why advocacy is so powerful.*

CH 4 - GET KNOWN WITHOUT SPENDING A FORTUNE

Now, we all advocate in one way or another. But the question is, are you advocating in a way that is consistent, and that delivers the best result for everyone? Regarding what you do advocate for well, can others tell clearly, what it is you are doing? Ultimately people are asking the question:

Are you FOR or AGAINST me and my life?

You want to be for. David Dawkins from Wells Fargo Advisors refers to financial advisors as "trusted advisors and dream makers." I believe that. I think the FA who embraces the concepts of this book will have the perspective to be the best advisor on the street. I think that's why my clients want to hear from me.

In this chapter, I'm going to talk about a mostly *overlooked* philanthropic vehicle that can align your personal vision and values with your clients' and the community, and subsequently, build advocacy for your brand and your practice.

This will help you *control marketing dollars* that will benefit everyone. It's a win-win. And, it's a great way to become known and to *promote* your community, and religious and philanthropic interests that express your values and who you really are. Since your practice is a natural extension of you, it's a great method to use to promote your practice without having to spend a fortune.

I want to be clear that there is not a "quid quo pro" or a "pay to play" implied here. I am suggesting that you support efforts that are important to you, your clients and your community.

I – Donor Advised Funds

This is a statement I think you could find useful when you are meeting with individuals and organizations that you share a common charitable interest with:

> *"I would love to consider recommending a grant for your organization from my charitable entity, but first I need to learn more about its work, 501c3 status and consider my funding budget for the year."*

But what do you need to do to be able to make a statement like that? And why is that statement so powerful? Let's explore this.

First, I'm going to introduce the vehicle called a *Donor Advised Fund* (DAF). What is it? It's a public charity. But it's treated like a mutual fund. Put simply, when the money goes into the DAF (if you have one), you may be entitled to a tax deduction, and you can control where the money goes through a grant recommendation process.

Note: Tax benefits depend upon your client's individual circumstances. You should consult a Tax Advisor. Donations cannot be revoked. The Board of Directors of the Gift Funds have ultimate control over all assets. Donor Advised Donors do not receive investment returns. The amount ultimately available for Donor directed grants may be more or less than Donor contributions to the Donor Advised Fund. While annual giving is encouraged, the Donor Advised Fund should be viewed as a long-term philanthropic program. While the operations of the Donor Advised Fund and its Pooled Income Funds are regulated by the Internal Revenue Service, they are not guaranteed or insured by the United States or any of its agencies or instrumentalities. Contributions are not insured by the FDIC and are not deposits or other obligations of, or guaranteed by, any depository institution.

For example, I sat on the investment board of a university foundation. I didn't go to that university, nor were they a client, but I have respected and benefited from the fine work of the university.

A fund of $5,000 or so had been established through numerous small contributions from a law enforcement trade organization. So, I did a little research and found out the university only creates a spending account for endowments with a balance of $40,000. That's a *discrepancy* of $35,000.

Guess what I did? I started figuring out how we can go about *rallying troops* to find $35,000 and most of it came from my families' DAF. Now, how does that make you look in the community? You are not only viewed with respect by the named trade group but by the university and other community organizations as well. The key is that once the fund reaches the $40,000 threshold, it can begin paying out the 4% spending account.

When you work like that, when you serve a *cause*, I can tell you that people come from out of the woodwork and say, "Yeah, we need to get behind this." In this case, my interest and leadership started a $1,500 annual scholarship distribution to help members of underrepresented racial minority groups with a preference for African Americans with an interest in working in correctional or criminal justice agencies. Based on the most recent university report, $12,000 in scholarships have been awarded.

With a DAF, your status in the community will be elevated. But don't do it just for the status. Do it because you are clear on what you care about. Let your DAF be an expression of that.

When you participate in this manner: the community wins, and you can win, too. Why? Because like I said, you can approach an organization and say, *"I would love to consider recommending a grant for your organization from my charitable entity, but first I need to learn more about its work, 501c3 status and consider our funding budget for the year."*

Do I tell the client in this case that I have $5,000 or $100,000 in the fund? No. That's a positioning statement. But at the next community event, as has happened in many cases in the past, I am positioned as a gentleman who wrote the check for a cause.

For example, I've been supporting programs that focus on young African Americans because of the experience I had at an HBCU (Historically Black Colleges and Universities) 40+ years ago. I've been doing this my whole professional life. I get charged up. Once on a business trip, when I learned that a major St. Louis firm was granting scholarships to the business school of a local HBCU I wanted to partner up with them immediately.

I committed to recommending a $750 grant to support the efforts. That amount won't change my life, but it might make a huge difference for a young person struggling to pay tuition. Where'd I get the money to fund the DAF?

CH 4 - GET KNOWN WITHOUT SPENDING A FORTUNE

Out of my profit margin. That's advertising you get to control. You can direct that expenditure 100%. You're not begging. You're negotiating. This is something we can do to demonstrate leadership for good causes that matter to us, our families, clients, and their community.

Imagine walking up to your branch manager and saying, *"We're doing this, but I'd like you to present the check. Can you give me another $750 and we'll do $1,500 together?"* That's an easy conversation to have. I suspect most branch managers are going to say, "I'm in there with you."

Why? Because they get to talk. They get to promote what they are doing in their marketplace and how their efforts benefit the community. *That's called partnership.*

Try that at your next community event and see what happens. In this case, I was introduced to the whole community with a statement like, "Mark Purnell, stand up. This is the guy who wrote the check for $750."

I'll give you another example. The National Association of Black Accountants is a group I have been associated with my whole professional life. They were going to Chicago for their national convention. Our firm, at the time, was headquartered in Chicago.

I thought we should be the $50,000 *platinum sponsor* for the event. So, I approached our head of the private client group (our chairman ended up being the keynote speaker) and said:

> *"David, we need to do this. We have three budget years. I will have $25,000 at the end of the three budget years. Can you*

> *match that? Because I know you can. The bigger question is can you get our chairman to protect the date on his calendar to deliver the keynote?"*

It didn't take long for him to say, "It's done, Mark."

Negotiate, don't beg.

At that time, our firm was involved in several merger transactions. And our chairman loved talking about that event in front of all the accountants at their national convention. This strategy works with your branch manager. You want to look for marketing dollars without having to spend a personal fortune.

What's a meaningful cause you want to serve? What's a meaningful cause your client serves? What's a mission close to your heart? What's a mission close to their heart? Your contribution to community and cause and business development don't have to be separate. They work together.

I love going to organizations my clients are involved in that I want to be involved in and saying, *"I'll be your matching fund.* Whatever you do. You raise $1,000, and I'll match it." I didn't have to go anywhere. I didn't have to ask the branch manager. How do I come off in the eyes of the client? You are elevated in the community and become known as a person people should get to know.

For example, I once had a client who said, "We'd like $1,000 to support an urban farm in Milwaukee." They'd been working with Michelle Obama on a national basis, and we wanted to encourage their efforts.

CH 4 - GET KNOWN WITHOUT SPENDING A FORTUNE

I said, "Great. I'll get the branch manager to present the check for $1,000." I went to the branch manager, and I said, "I need you to speak at this Milwaukee charity event. I got the $1,000 covered. Can you cover the food and beverage?" His response? "Done."

Clients and prospects from Wisconsin were at that event, but we shared the news with clients we serve in 34 states. We wanted *everyone* to know what we were doing to support a community project. This is how you effortlessly joint market with your manager, and with your client, and their philanthropic interests.

This is the kind of elevation you can achieve, and you don't have to wait for someone else's approval to do it. It's a key to being viewed as the client's advocate because you can control your charitable budget, who you're talking to, what you're supporting, and you have a pool of money you can direct.

Remember the business development budget? When you're investing in your business and elevating your status in the community, don't be afraid to go into your pocket and invest in your franchise business.

In conclusion, there are three ways we have discussed using a DAF:

First, by asking your branch manager to match your grant.

Second, by using your DAF to match your clients' philanthropic interests and perhaps the organization's efforts.

In the latter case, you are gaining more visibility by working with the organization to develop a fund-raising campaign which typically gives you a higher level of visibility and possibly board of directors' interaction. Finally, you can use a combination of both.

II – Why Every Advisor Ought to Know About and Use Guidestar.Org and 990 Filings

What does Guidestar.org let you do? And what's a 990 Filing? Guidestar.org is the world's largest source of information on non-profit organizations. 990 filings are informational tax forms most tax-exempt organizations must file annually. The form gives the IRS an overview of the organization's activities, governance, and detailed financial information.

It also includes a section where the organization outlines its accomplishments in the previous year, to justify and maintain its tax-exempt status. This information is available *for free* on Guidestar.org based on the "Freedom of Information Act."

What does knowing this let you do? Say you walk into a meeting for a client's not-for-profit, and you hold their 990 forms in your hand, a form they didn't give you. Someone in that meeting is going to respond, "Where'd you get that?" And you're going to say, "I got it off the public website. But what I want to talk about are the levels of where you're spending your money, and how your fundraisers are performing..."

How is that perceived by everyone? Impressive. But it also positions your client to advocate for you when you are not in the room. It's a subtle suggestion that maybe you can help in other financial areas.

Additionally, if you already know it is a cause you are aligned with, you can position what we discussed previously:

"I'll be your matching fund. Whatever you do, I'll match it. When is the next event going to be held?"

Not only are you showing you are advocating for your client's philanthropic interests, but you are also raising your status in the community, as you build greater advocacy for your practice and services.

It's back to the principle of doing your homework *ahead* of time and then advocating for all the key people involved. The eyes and ears in that room are going to be advocating for you and your practice, too.

I can't repeat this enough: You're advocating for the client. You're advocating for your partner advisors, too. You're advocating for the community. And, how much does it cost to use Guidestar.Org and 990 Filings? *Nothing*.

III - Your Homework: Set Up Your DAF

You can start a donor advice fund for $5,000. Your grants can be as little as $50. My fund is called the "Meet Me in The Kitchen" fund.

You know why? Back in the day, that's where everything used to happen for yellow-pad financial planners. I don't walk in through the front door. When I go out to see a client, I always come in through the kitchen because that's where business is done.

How to get started:

1. Determine your annual budget for funding your DAF with your CPA/tax advisor

2. Determine your annual spending/grant recommendation budget

3. Name your DAF, i.e., "Your Name Community Gift Fund"

4. Determine its purpose, e.g., "provide opportunities for the youth of your city"

5. Tell your top 10 clients about steps 1-4 above and ask if they are aware of any opportunities for you to consider for a grant recommendation

6. Tell your branch manager about steps 1-4 above and ask if they are aware of any opportunities for you to consider for a grant recommendation

7. Tell your top 10 prospects about steps 1-4 above and ask if they are aware of any opportunities for you to consider for a grant recommendation

8. Remember this statement and use it often *"I would love to consider recommending a grant for your organization from my charitable entity, but first I need to learn more about its work, 501c3 status and consider my funding budget for the year."*

CHAPTER 5:

Grow Your Business Without Burning Out

"The work you do while you procrastinate is probably the work you should be doing for the rest of your life."
– Jessica Hische

ATTAINING CLIENTS IS ONE thing. Building upon your existing client base and extending your practice to the next level is another. Doing all it takes to acquire the right clients, retain them, and sustain your practice is by no means a small undertaking. It's not uncommon to end up being burnt out.

One of the critical ways to avoid burn out is to have an aligned team, and systems in place that help you do what you don't want to do, and what you don't have time to do for yourself.

Providing a personalized financial service to the mass affluent market makes it difficult to keep all the functions in a nice and neat box or function chart.

In marketing and financial services, mass affluent and emerging affluent are the high end of the mass market, or individuals with US$100,000 to US$1,000,000 of liquid financial assets, or consumers with an annual household income over US$75,000.

Industry experts and coaches like Bill Good (author of *Hot Prospects: The Proven Prospecting System to Ramp Up Your Sales Career*) who started coaching me in 1985 and Mark Wood, Practice Management Director at a major investment firm, agree these basic functions can be performed effectively by a sole practitioner for a $300,000 practice in the mass affluent market.

Serving the high-net-worth individual, (as defined in the Western and primarily American private banking business market) presents additional challenges. In Western, and the primarily American private banking businesses, these individuals typically are defined as having investable finance (financial assets, excluding primary residence) of more than US$1 million. Because of this, they would have more complex needs and require a wider set of skills and service team members.

When the wealth is around $5 million, she/he is then referred to as "very HNWI." In cases where the wealth is more than $30 million, the person is classified as "ultra HNWI."[5]

In this chapter, I am going to cover more about the different roles in a team, a topic we touched on earlier. But I am also going to share what each of these roles *ought* to be doing in comparison to what they shouldn't be doing. More importantly, in making that clear, I hope to help you identify *what* you should be focusing more of your time on, and what you should be engaging or hiring help for.

Remember, you can't do this all alone. A successful practice requires teamwork. While it is not easy to build a team from scratch, especially if you are starting with limited funds to invest in hiring full-time help, it is also *necessary* if you want to build and sustain a thriving practice.

Here are a few observations that may surprise you based on Bill Good's research (from his book *Hot Prospects*) and based on my work with my coaching clients; they are still valid today.

First, an estimated 30% to 40% of an adviser's time is spent satisfying "client demands" or wearing the service hat/function (i.e., answering questions such as, "When is my check going to arrive?"). Second, the advisor works to understand the client, their issues and concerns and develops client-centered strategies. Coordinating those strategies across their assets with internal and external advisors is probably worth close to *$1,000 per hour*.

---

5 Staff, Investopedia. "High Net Worth Individual - HNWI." Investopedia. January 20, 2016. Accessed February 04, 2018. https://www.investopedia.com/terms/h/hnwi.asp.

CH 5 - GROW YOUR BUSINESS WITHOUT BURNING OUT

It doesn't take much analysis to reach the conclusion that to become more efficient: an advisor should buy back 30-40% of their day and figure out how to spend more time with clients who are decent people and follow your advice.

Buying that time back, unfortunately, is not easy today and it was my first challenge in 1985. You typically can't buy time back on a part-time basis; you have to buy it on a full-time basis.

Starting out, you must focus on your clients and all the main roles in your business, so you can understand what is needed, and begin to find what "hats" bring you the most joy, sense of satisfaction, and accomplishment. Get more face time with prospects and clients and then get *better* face time.

Once you build a $300,000 practice, you can start hiring to go to the next level[6]. Let me tell you here that you will need to begin building a team before you think you can comfortably afford it. If you already have a practice in the millions, then this chapter will help you decide how much funding you need to put into a team.

According to a study by Vanguard-Spectrum, clients leave their advisors for four main reasons:

1. Long-term portfolio losses;

2. Not being proactive in contacting the client;

---

[6] Good, Bill. "Ten Mistakes in Team Building." ThinkAdvisor. July 26, 2011. Accessed February 04, 2018. http://www.thinkadvisor.com/2011/07/26/ten-mistakes-in-team-building.

3. Not providing the client with good ideas/advice; and

4. Not returning phone calls/emails in a timely manner.

As I mentioned previously, most financial advisors wear three hats. You need to attract new clients/develop new business opportunities, maintain a relationship with the client, and manage/oversee portfolio decisions and outcomes. Let's review these roles again.

1. **Business development manager.** A business development manager works to improve an organization's market position and achieve financial growth.

2. **Relationship manager.** A relationship manager is a professional who works to improve a firm's relationships with both partner firms and customers. I spend most my time in this role. I advocate for all my staff, partner advisors, clients, and the important people in their lives.

3. **Portfolio manager.** A portfolio manager is a person or group of people responsible for investing assets, implementing investment strategy, and managing day-to-day portfolio trading.

Some observers would blur these clear lines by adding technology hats/functions, marketing hats/functions, and satisfying "client demands" service hat/functions. But I believe in *supporting* these three basic functions. I like to keep it simple and stick to three. It's easier to remember.

CH 5 - GROW YOUR BUSINESS WITHOUT BURNING OUT

Back to my point. Subsequently (and to no surprise), the main reasons clients leave their advisors corresponds with failures in the three main roles we covered above, and more importantly, a failure in the way they *coordinate* and stay *client-centered*.

You all must advocate. You can have managers who are great at each of these roles, but they might be terrible at working together. This doesn't bode well for your clients.

I'll cover more about how a high-performing team needs to function in the next chapter, how to bring that harmony to other advisors on your client's team, and more importantly, how to become the *Gatekeeper* for your clients' affairs.

In looking at the three key roles, which one is the most natural for you? Which one do you enjoy? Below I discuss more about the roles, and what they entail, so you can decide the one you want to focus on. For the rest, you must either hire or partner up.

Let's talk again about gaining access to information that will make you a better advisor and perhaps greatly enhance the value of your practice. How do you add someone to your internal advisory team? My friend, Bill Good, does a great job of describing the difference between a coach and a teacher. I think it's important to insert the idea of engaging an outside consultant, mentor or advisor here because it will save you a lot of time and money to help you assemble a team.

Bill puts it like this:

Do you need a coach?

Whether you are interested in executive coaching, sales coaching, or even life coaching, let's first make certain we know exactly what the term "coach" means.

The concept is simple, but it must be understood in relation to another term, "teacher."

Teacher: One who imparts knowledge to others, usually in a structured school situation, but also on a more informal basis.

Coach: One who helps others implement knowledge gained to the point where it constitutes a skill.

A coach, especially a good one, takes what you know, frequently adds to it, but focuses on getting you to apply it, and thereby become better at your particular skill.

So, an acting coach would obviously work with an actor to help his or her performance.

A golf coach might push, cajole, encourage, and provide feedback, all for the purpose of improving skills that ultimately improve the game.

A business coach, in my opinion, should focus on getting the student to do what successful people do, and not what unsuccessful people do. The end result: good coaching results in continuous improvement.

Do you need a "coach" to help you assemble a team?

Well, I sure did.

CH 5 - GROW YOUR BUSINESS WITHOUT BURNING OUT

I have used these two firms to help me assemble teams:

>The Training Connection, Inc.
>4004 Genesee Place, Suite 109
>Prince William, VA 22192

And:

>Paragon Resources, Inc.
>P.O. Box 724705
>Atlanta, GA 31139

These firms have both embraced the use of the:

>*"Success Insights Wheel"*

The Success Insights Wheel Is a visual guide to gauge how people relate to each other and their environment. You can quickly see an imbalance in a group or team requiring ALL types of people to fulfill ALL aspects of the job/business required for success.

Using a consulting firm along with this tool and methodology can produce a huge return on investment when assembling your team of professionals.

I have included my wheel, and you can see adding teammates that plotted in the analyzer, coordinator, supporter, relater or C & S section of the wheel would complement my adopted and natural skill set.

A TRUSTED FINANCIAL ADVISOR

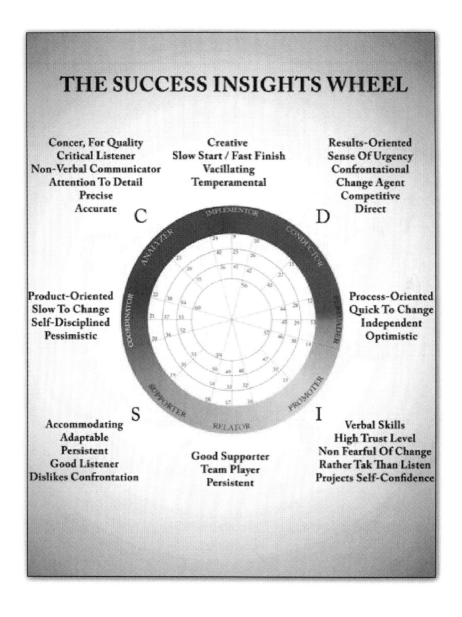

CH 5 - GROW YOUR BUSINESS WITHOUT BURNING OUT

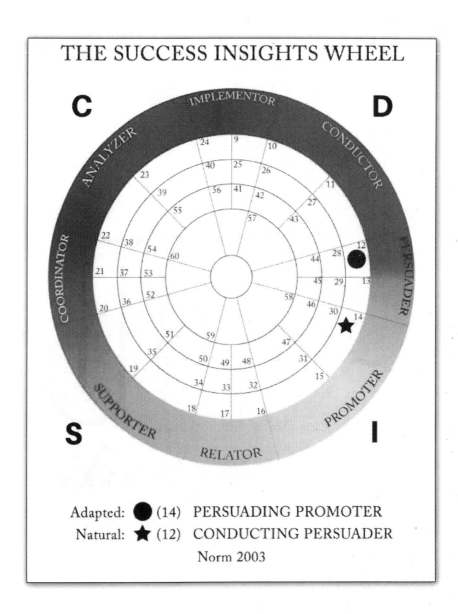

I - The Business Development Manager

Successful business development managers do many things. Their focus is to seek out opportunities for more business and find ways to formulize them. Activities could include:

Attending conferences and meetings where potential clients are, or where key people are who will lead to potential clients.

- Facilitating and meeting sales calls quotas
- Delivering sales presentations to key stakeholders
- Managing marketing activities such as promotional content and paid advertising

The list of activities can be many. But a good business development manager must <u>have a clearly defined</u> niche market. I'll cover more about that topic later in this chapter.

A niche is a *focused target market* that is understood well and subsequently informs how other functions need to serve that niche. We touched on this concept in Chapter 1 when we discussed what *high-net-worth clients* want and expect from their advisors.

I found that I work especially well with Family Stewards, business owners (particularly CPAs, as that was my background), and women who have *strong* community interests.

CH 5 - GROW YOUR BUSINESS WITHOUT BURNING OUT

Why? These investors with substantial assets realize they are *blessed* and feel *fortunate* to have accumulated a large amount of money. They aren't concerned with making that pile bigger. They are concerned with how they can use that money to be a support to those who are *less fortunate*.

I realized, something about my mentality, personality, and approach appealed to them. They are a very tight network of people. So, when word got around about my work, and how I advocate for everyone involved and keep their interests first in mind, introductions and invitations to be involved in planning sessions with community leaders and potential clients became routine occurrences. This allowed me to get a lot more done in less time.

The great news about finding a niche? Once you establish yourself, word of mouth spreads reducing your cost of strong advertising investment or the like. Better yet, because you can serve so many clients in your practice at one time, your perceived value increases, too. So, it is easier to *raise your rates* if you would like.

Serving a niche means you build deep expertise and experience in that area. Over time, your practice develops specialized knowledge that isn't easily copied or replaced. So, not only do you become a practice or advisor everyone raves about, but you and your practice become a business where niche clients *crave* to engage.

I noticed when I placed myself in the role of business development manager with a niche; I could focus on doing very small, targeted events. I haven't had a lot of success hosting a happy hour and inviting all my clients. They don't feel special.

Whereas, if you have a targeted event, most of your clients will know each other. They know who is attending, and they feel special because you planned it just for them.

If you have a clear niche, it is like having 20/20 vision on the bullseye. If you don't, building your business is at best, wishful shooting.

Here is a summary of traits a natural business development manager has:

- Communication skills. You must be good at communicating with people, making them feel comfortable, making them feel it's *OK* to share things that society says you don't talk about, like money and debt. So, having the ability to get them to open up a little bit is important.

- A love to be out of the office with the public (e.g., office, business, and public places), and are comfortable talking to strangers in many varied and different settings and environments.

- A love of learning about the topic of financial affairs and the life affairs of your niche. Why? So, you can speak with them about a range of topics and recognize when issues or opportunities arise. For example, I don't prepare taxes, nor do I handle estate planning, but I'm knowledgeable enough, so the client doesn't need a complete team of resources. You can have one person with good knowledge of different areas."

- A focus on results. They have a clear direction and can help people arrive at a decision.

II - The Relationship Manager

The subject of great service is so vast, but here are the basics:

- Moments of truth are resolved quickly and to the client's satisfaction
- Communicates with other advisory team members (e.g., CPA)
- Great service is fast
- Great service solves the right problem correctly
- Great service is meticulous in follow-up
- Great service is friendly
- Great service is delivered by a service professional

Going by the basics, you will notice how the relationship manager's capacity to execute these objectives properly also helps with business development. The three main functions are inseparable to one another. They complement one another. If one fails, they all fail. That's why being *coordinated* is so critical.

At least one member of your relationship management team should be a team member who acts as a liaison between the client and the other team members. Their job, like an expeditor[7] in a restaurant, is to ensure that client

---

[7] The expeditor serves as a liaison between the wait staff of the restaurant and the restaurant cook. They ensure that all kitchen orders are prepared in a timely manner and according to the

requests are fulfilled in a timely manner, paperwork is handled properly, and the standards of the team and firm are met and upheld. This should include returning phone calls and emails promptly.

The more personal a relationship you have with a client, the more they will value that relationship, and the less likely they will want to leave. I've found that participating in family celebrations and events of significant importance is one of the best ways to build personal relationships. Attend retirement functions, funerals, graduations, and other family gatherings when invited.

Here is a summary of traits a natural relationship manager has:

- Communication is key. It's not about you. You must take yourself out of the equation. You can't have an ego. It must be about them and their needs, first and foremost.

- A love for inclusion and harmony. Where there is tension or conflict between personnel, it can be democratic, take both sides into account, and bring multiple parties to an understanding.

- A grounded personality. They can see the forest from the trees. Where visionary thinkers and drivers want to move faster than the speed of light, relationship managers slow things down, so no one else on the team is left out.

---

restaurant menu and customer specifications. https://www.snagajob.com/job-descriptions/food-expeditor.

CH 5 - GROW YOUR BUSINESS WITHOUT BURNING OUT

Put simply, if you were hiring a relationship manager, the team member would emphasize INCLUSION, provide STABILITY, use SINCERITY and bring HARMONY.

III - The Portfolio Manager

The portfolio manager is also known as the investment or assets manager. If you are a portfolio manager, you will generally be focusing on, these components in your philosophy or work style:

- You need to have an investment strategy that will protect your clients from another 2000 or 2008. If you don't, the next market meltdown will likely erode your clients' retirement savings and set your own practice back years. This strategy will be documented as a financial plan. It doesn't need to be an elaborate document. It can be as simple as stating the client's goals and needs, and the basic steps you will take to satisfy them.

- You need to explain your investment strategy in a concise and conversational way. Why? Because if your clients can't understand it, it's unlikely they will fully trust you. It is important to annually review the plan and to invite the client to this review. The relationship management team can help with this as well.

- Your investment strategy should be based on the ethos of "putting clients' best interests first." The investment strategy you implement must meet (even exceed) the client's goals and objectives. It must also be executed in a manner where potential conflicts are disclosed before they become a problem.

Remember, the client is hiring you to do for them what they can't do for themselves. Portfolio managers free cli-

CH 5 - GROW YOUR BUSINESS WITHOUT BURNING OUT

ents from the burden of making day-to-day investment decisions, and the complexities required to make *effective decisions*. Such as being very attuned to the market.

A bad investment can destroy client relationships. But as we've already seen, sound investment advice alone is not enough to retain clients.

Typically, if the portfolio grows under the investment manager's stewardship, the manager is compensated by receiving a *higher dollar amount* as the management fee (% of returns). This reduces the adviser's temptation to "churn" the account to generate more commissions—a major flaw of a transaction-based investment model.

Don't be a product pusher. Become out-of-the-box and solution-oriented, not sales-oriented. Because these people have seen every sales strategy you're ever going to try. They're looking for guidance in creating a team approach; they don't want to be sold an annuity, product, a life insurance policy or anything similar. *You are the product.*

My observations have led me to realize that if I maintained the discretionary trading authority as an advisor, I would need to spend a *great amount of time* in this role of portfolio management and trading. The other two hats, I enjoy and am more attuned to fulfilling, suffered. I had to come to terms with that.

Is portfolio management for you? Here are the traits I would typically look for if I were hiring a portfolio manager:

- Portfolio managers tend to want to stay in the office and work alone. This doesn't mean they don't care about people. Their workstyle is more introverted, product-oriented and slow to change.

- Portfolio managers are detail oriented, and can sort out what could go wrong, so they can develop a strategy that accounts for risky and unlikely events.

- Portfolio managers emphasize accuracy, analysis, and logic to make decisions and provide advice.

IV - Homework: What Hat Should You Wear?

This exercise will help you determine what hat you should be wearing most of the time. Do a time study of a typical day in your workweek. Now, answer the following questions:

- **What** activities do you do?
- **When** do you do these activities?
- **What**, out of these activities, do you **enjoy** doing?
- **Why** do you enjoy it?
- What activities that you do, **don't you enjoy**?
- What activities **energize you**?
- What activities **drain your energies**?

Now based on your understanding of the three roles, identify one or two where you should be focusing *most* of your time.

Second, engage a firm to help you conduct a team building assessment. Use this tool with existing team members as well as potential team members. Don't bring on a new team member at any level without this personal assessment and a team mapping.

What is a team building assessment? The TTI Success Insights® tool for example[8], is a user-friendly assessment tool designed to help employees understand the value they bring to the team.

The TTI Success Insights® report clarifies individual work styles, how styles affect job performance and how the team can work together to build on strengths, overcome weaknesses and improve overall organizational effectiveness. A personalized report details:

- Basic Characteristics
- Work Characteristics
- Value to the Team
- Value to the Organization
- Effective Communication
- Don'ts on Communicating
- Communication Tips
- Team Effectiveness Factors
- Perceptions
- Descriptors
- Action Plan
- Style Insights Graphs/The Success Insights® Wheel

---

8 "Team Building Assessments." The Training Connection, Inc. Accessed February 04, 2018. http://www.thetrainingconnection.com/team-assessments.php.

SECTION III:
Secure Clients For Life

CHAPTER 6:

A Fast Track To Rapid Growth

*"He who knows others is learned.
He who knows himself is wise."*
— Lao Tzu

HAVING A NICHE IS like knowing *exactly* where to dig to find gold. Not having a niche is like digging a hole in any substance that looks like dirt in the hopes you'll find something of value. In the last chapter, I discussed the power of niche markets, and why every business development manager should have one. The benefits to your practice are innumerable. I'll share more on that in this chapter.

Over the years, a key niche market for me was CPAs who were of African American descent, because my background was in accounting and I'm African American myself. But that wasn't a niche. My niche was found within the families of that market; I also worked with Family Stewards who are predominantly female (unique in the advisory business), and who wanted to put their dollars to use to support a cause. Their husbands generated the money. They helped decide how to put it to use.

Your niche doesn't have to be perfectly identified. You will be passionate about your niche, you can create a client profile for it, and you can narrow and focus your brand around it, making it known so others can refer potential clients to you. Specifically, you can focus on large employers in your area, financial products like annuities or municipal bonds, life transitions involving marriage or divorce and finally money-in-motion resulting from retirement, inheritance or selling a business.

I – Define Your Niche

Since my focus in this book is to show you how to secure high-net-worth clients and how to thrill them and incite them to rave about your work, I will share my thinking and how I used the "occupational niche."

I was a consultant and worked for two international accounting firms before becoming a financial advisor. So, I was very knowledgeable and comfortable with accounting service providers.

Because of my experience in the field, I understood the psychographics, demographics, and their unique challenges. Consequently, I was easily accepted and had high creditability.

How did this come to be? I believe that people like doing business and working with people that look like them and think like them. That's not a racial statement or a gender statement. But it's something to consider when you look at what your niche is or can be.

Think about how you and your team members or partners think and act in the world. Who is it you naturally attract to your business?

I relate to women because I understand they typically don't have a voice; this is similar to how African Americans don't typically have a voice. I relate to Family Stewards because I care about my family. I relate to CPAs (even though I'm not a CPA) because I wanted to be a CPA in a former life.

Birds of a feather flock together...those of similar tastes congregate in groups.

Working in a niche market has a lot of benefits. First, you can specialize. Advisers who are specialists, and possess an expertise, can solve problems for a select group of people. Your specialization makes you and your firm more attractive than other advisers offering general services to a broader audience. Why? You make a *specialized group of people* feel special. You make them feel like your practice was designed for them.

You may already have a niche. You may think you don't. In that case, it is worth your time to look at your client-base, especially the clients you enjoy working with and the ones who respond to you well. Doing so will allow you to try to identify a few trends. You can easily confirm your niche, through demographic data, for example. But you also need to account for what's not so easily observable, such as *mindset* and *way of thinking* (psychographics). Either way, it is worth surveying.

Why? Because you can *tailor* your messaging. Let me give you an example. If you can communicate effectively with CPAs, your clients will love you because they're intimate, and trust the CPA. If you have a good working relationship with the CPA, they are very excited and thrilled to know that fact.

When I talk with a CPA, I want them to know I am interested in their practice and that I want to support their efforts with our mutual clients. A lot of CPAs are quiet people, but they do big things for their clients.

Advocating for the CPA with your mutual client(s) goes a long way and looking for opportunities to promote additional work and opportunities for the CPA is always valued and appreciated. You might ask yourself, *what is the niche market of the CPA?*

Having a niche makes business development, relationship management, and portfolio management much more streamlined.

Having a niche provides focus for your practice.

When you create a profile around your target market, and you tailor your message to them, you might hit on opportunities specific to an occupation, or hobbies, and interests, or specialized planning needs.

I have found my high-net-worth women clients tend to have strong philanthropic interests, and value multigenerational wealth planning. They think about how their children or grandchildren will manage, benefit, and protect the family assets.

I tend to focus on providing educational opportunities and encourage conversation in these areas. I will share articles, offer lessons learned from other clients as well as suggest a "bonus service" (a complimentary offering) to sit in on any telephone or face-to-face meeting with a client and their outside advisors.

Some advisors say:

> *"I do three things. I specialize in accumulating assets, helping my clients grow their assets. I specialize in distributi-*

CH 6 - A FAST TRACK TO RAPID GROWTH

> *on and getting income from those assets, and I specialize in getting the assets to the next generation."*

These are the three major areas. But you can specialize in one area. This area can be segmented to allow your *growth specialist*, *income specialist*, and *generational planning specialist* within your team, to cover all three bases.

Then, your practice looks more attractive to a high-net-worth client, because you can take them through all three of those phases, or whatever phase they happen to be in at the time.

You can specifically tailor your message, and your marketing, to address those needs. Certainly, once you've done that, you can showcase the rest of your expertise in this area of investment planning, and planning needs to an audience; you can, over time, catalyze more word of mouth, and build your reputation as a trusted resource in that area. You can also write specialized papers about it and speak about their topic of interest. The possibilities are endless.

When you narrow your service, you become quite efficient, because you have a good process, and you've targeted your market; you can enhance your profitability of the practice.

When you focus on clients who have specialized but similar investment and planning needs, there are many benefits. Streamlining permits you to free up time and resources to properly customize solutions for your clients. Why? Because your client's needs, the way they think, and

A TRUSTED FINANCIAL ADVISOR

the way they generally want someone to operate, is *very similar*.

The question is: when you have a niche does it mean you are making a risky business decision by concentrating your practice in a narrow market? Surely there must be drawbacks, right? Not really. But there are a few distinctions. Especially in the advisory practice. Remember, no one ever stays in one niche forever.

Why? People age and the money flows from owner to their successors, a topic I covered in Chapter 1. When you focus on a niche, you are also looking at *who will part-take* in that niche in the future, and *who will exit* that niche in the future. In other words, a niche can be *diversified across time*.

But if there was one major drawback, it is that you are probably going to have some clients that *don't meet your niche criteria*. This is a natural part of business, and it is necessary at times to accommodate them to build your practice. Eventually, you will want to focus 100% on your niche.

Say you specialize in serving corporate executives, what do you do when a client *isn't* a corporate executive? Well, you must be careful. Because you are knowledgeable about this niche, you will need a more general process in place to serve this client. You don't want to assume their needs are the same as your other clientele.

In other words, I'm saying it's easy to assume a client is concerned about their taxes because that's my specialty. I always want to know who the CPA is, and whether can we work together. If that's not important to the client who doesn't fit the niche profile, if they're more concerned about their estate plan, or how their kids are going to inherit their money, you want to make sure your process accommodates that.

You've got to have a process that's broad enough, so you will meet your clients' needs.

Now here's the catch. Even though you work in a niche market, that's no excuse to get lazy on customization. Why? Because no matter how niche you get, every client is still like a snowflake. It's important to remember that.

You could have two engineers, and one of them might be very detail-oriented, while the other might focus on the big picture. You want to make sure that you're servicing and concerned about their needs as well as communicating to them in a manner that addresses their needs; provide details for the detailed person and paint the big picture for the big-picture person.

II – When to Say No

Lastly, let's talk about saying no to a potential client because they don't fit your needs or your market niche. I've had to turn down clients during the on-boarding process. The potential client needs to understand why you can't work with them.

Why?

By articulating your rationale, you lay the groundwork for a future possible relationship when circumstances change.

1. They need to know that the arrangement can improve their situation and help them meet their goals and visions.
2. You need to know if the arrangement can help them meet their goals *and* whether the arrangement will be beneficial to your practice and existing clientele.

I'll reference the above two points with an example. One of my best clients referred a business partner of theirs, and I really wanted to do business with them. We had good chemistry, but I had to turn the client down because their other adviser (a portfolio manager) was retiring, so that's why they were looking for a new adviser. But I didn't possess the expertise they needed.

They wanted to talk directly to their portfolio manager before trades would be done. They enjoyed that interaction with their investment adviser. I could tell it was a very important part of their relationship.

CH 6 - A FAST TRACK TO RAPID GROWTH

My value I bring to the table is that I delegate the day-to-day portfolio management to a private manager, or to a mutual fund. *Although they wanted me to be "that guy," I couldn't. They wanted me for the job, not my portfolio manager.*

That process would not have worked well. I could have found an external portfolio manager who could meet with the client on a quarterly basis, a portfolio manager who was near, so that they could communicate. But in this case, I could not get a good fit, and I had made a practice decision several years earlier not to have an internal portfolio manager.

I demonstrated to the prospect where I thought we could help and the related benefits, and that we should keep the door open to the possibility of working together in the future.

The next point is: what *impact* will the new client have on your existing clientele and your practice overall? Because you're already working at your full capacity, you shouldn't bring in a client that would influence your service quality to diminish. That's not good for your reputation, and it is also an irresponsible move to make as it *deters* you from placing your existing clients' needs as the priority.

Again, every decision you make in your practice, including who you take on as a client and who you don't take on, has ramifications for everyone involved. These decisions can demonstrate you are advocating for your clients' needs, or that you are not. They will either 1) appreciate the value of your brand and strengthen your advocacy in the market, or 2) they will dilute it.

III - Homework: Identify Your Niche

Look at your existing (top 20) clients, and identify patterns in response to the following questions:

- What are their big concerns? Use the spreadsheet below.
- What are their major fears?
- What do you solve for them?
- What about you and/or your practice do they love most?
- What are their main philanthropic or monetary interests?
- Where does their money flow, and for what purpose?
- Where do they live?
- How old are they?
- Are they male or female?
- How big are their families?
- What is their income-bracket?
- Are there any ethnic trends?
- What is their main attitude toward life, including people in their lives, the community, and the world at large? (Said another way: what is their worldview?)
- Who are the key decision-makers in their lives?

CH 6 - A FAST TRACK TO RAPID GROWTH

- When you or your relationship manager meet with them informally, what topics (people, events, activities) do they love talking about most?

If you don't know the answers to any of the questions above, find out. Sometimes, it is as simple as asking your client. Then ask yourself the following questions:

- Can you marry your name to a financial product or strategy (i.e., become a product expert)?

- Are you a godsend to clients getting married, divorced, who are widowed or have a child?

- Have you been helpful to clients in retirement, changing jobs, gaining an inheritance?

- Do you enjoying working with business owners exiting their business?

- Are you knowledgeable about the benefits of a large employer in your area?

By the time you are done answering the questions above, you will start to get a *very clear picture* of your niche.

Value Provided Top 20 Clients

Philanthrophy	What do we Solve?	BIG Concerns	HH Name	First Name of Key	AUM	T12 Rev
Personal Foundation	Monitor other advisors	Becoming Poor Again			$0	$0
USGT-DAF	Inter-generational Planning	Taxes			$0	$0
USGT DAF	Reassurance of POR	Having Sounding Board			$0	$0
Humane Society	Reassurance of POR	Untimely Emotional Decisions			$0	$0
Golf Outing/Wells Fargo	Moments of Truth Advocacy	Exposure For Young AA Males			$0	$0
Church of God	Moments of Truth Advocacy	Intergenerational Planning			$0	$0
Summer Program	Moments of Truth Advocacy	Young Aspiring Accountants			$0	$0
Diabetes Interests	Inter-generational Planning	Suceesor Trustee			$0	$0
Cancer Interests	Reassurance of POR	Having Sounding Board			$0	$0
Education Interests	Reassurance of POR	Handling of Divorce Settlement			$0	$0
Local Community Foundation	Inter-generational Planning	Taxes			$0	$0

1 - Moment of Truth-In customer service, instance of contact or interaction between a customer and a firm that gives the customer an opportunity to form (or change) an impression about the firm

2-Reassurance of POR-Envision is current and result >80

CHAPTER 7:

A Step-By-Step Process To Secure High-Net-Worth Clients

"I have learned that success is to be measured not so much by the position that one has reached in life as by the obstacles which he has had to overcome while trying to succeed."
– Booker T. Washington

YOU MIGHT BE SURPRISED to hear that if you have read up to this point in the book, you *already* have the information you need to secure high-net-worth clients. In this chapter, I will apply all the elements you have learned from previous chapters, to enable you to secure high-net-worth clients.

If you already have high-net-worth clients, doing what I shared in Chapter 6 will help you secure even more of

CH 7 - SECURE HIGH-NET-WORTH CLIENTS

them. But what if you don't have high-net-worth accounts yet? What do you do? In this chapter, we'll cover exactly that. Had I known what I know today, what I am about to share with you is how I would have gone about securing such clients. And I would have certainly paid for access to this knowledge.

You will need to refer to your homework assignment from Chapter 5. Let's assume I have several significant and key connections and clients at "Casino," a Las Vegas employer with 13,000 employees. I have decided this a niche market for me, and I am looking to work with executives and employees of the "Casino."

If I specialized in working with Casino employees and you were a generalist, I would crush you in that market. Here is how I would do it:

1. Become well-versed in the Casino's healthcare, retirement plans, benefit packages, etc. and make myself known to everyone at the firm.

2. Create a free report for people retiring in the next five years, and book appointments to discuss those reports. I would also figure out if there's an employee newsletter and gather important news/findings.

3. Ask a few employees for informational interviews regarding their specific wants/needs. I would figure out the pros and cons of their current 401(k) plans and packages. Then I would use this information in my marketing, so people would understand I'm not just pretending to be an expert. Plus, the people I've

interviewed will start telling their friends how I'm the person who only works with Casino employees.

4. Find out what community and philanthropic interests are supported by the Casino and the interests of the key executives like UNLV, Bishop Gorman High School, Catholic Charities of Southern Nevada, Nevada Cancer Institute, Opportunity Village and St. Jude's Ranch, etc.

5. Arrange to sponsor an event, by partnering up, and look for ways to gain marketing dollars. We discussed this subject in Chapter 4.

Now, the Casino has over 13,000 employees. Even if I only converted 1% of the people, that's still 130 clients – nothing to sneeze at. If you're in Milwaukee, you can do the same with Kohl's Corp. If you're in Seattle, go after Amazon. Here's what you do:

- Figure out the largest employers in your area and carve out your niche. You can make a name for yourself by offering to hold free workshops for them and networking where their employees do. Once you get the ball rolling, you can deliver great value to your clients and procure co-worker referrals.

- Look for opportunities to align your Charitable Fund/ Donor Advised Fund.

Make sure the above information is available to your business development manager (which could be you). Speaking the language of your niche is the *first step* to building trust so you can get a face-to-face and more intimate meeting time with your potential client.

Now you are ready to meet with each of your clients (including your potential clients) and map out what's important to them. Especially their familial values, and their charitable interests. You can interview existing clients. Identify what charities are important to them. Here's a good interview format to use.

Please check the three items that are the most important to you.

- Retirement
    - Having enough income during retirement
    - Purchasing a retirement property or secondary residence
    - Providing for education of children or grandchildren
    - Determining when and how to withdraw funds from investments to provide for my retirement income
- Legacy and Estate Planning Strategies
    - Positioning myself to enjoy more of the things in life I value
    - Having a plan in place for my financial future
    - Making sure my family will be secure in the event of a catastrophe, e.g., dcath or disability of a breadwinner
    - Caring for elders or family with special needs

- Passing my estate to my heirs smoothly without court battles
- Protecting my estate from estate taxes and transfer costs
- Providing a legacy and financial resources for successor generations
- Providing capital for the charitable organizations I support
- Protecting my assets from creditors and liability lawsuits

- Cash Flow, Liabilities, and Investments
  - Restructuring or eliminating debt
  - Knowing where to put old and new investment funds
  - Understanding my liquidity needs now, and in the future
  - Having someone study my investment profile and make a recommendation on what type of portfolio I should have
  - Maximizing tax efficiency including reducing income taxes generated from my investments
  - Avoiding capital gains or excessive taxes on the sale of business interests or investments

Remember, you must study what's important to them as if it is just as important to you. You are adopting the client's vision and making it your own.

CH 7 - SECURE HIGH-NET-WORTH CLIENTS

After the meeting, update or create their investment plan and their net-worth statement. Pay attention to their entire net-worth statement including:

1. Assets
2. Liabilities
3. Insurance Needs
    a. Long-Term Care
    b. Life
    c. Healthcare
    d. Property & Casualty
4. Illiquid Assets
    a. Real Estate
    b. Business Interests
    c. Other Emotional Assets

Determine how you and your team (if you have one) can meet their specific needs and present your plan to the client as an offering. To do this, I would fully embrace Al Dudley's (Wells Fargo Advisor) methodology for on-boarding clients by instituting a process that benefits an advisor in several ways. The process is so involved it needs three meetings to cover the entirety.

The first meeting allows us to discuss our firm and how we serve clients using a holistic approach. We gather background information and what's important to the client. It's really a "fit" meeting and determines if we will have the chemistry for a second meeting.

The second meeting is designed to gather all the data required to review their situation and assess if we can make any recommendations that could benefit the client and improve their situation.

The third meeting gives us the opportunity to deliver our findings and recommendations. This is where we present our proposal to the prospect and offer them the opportunity to become our client.

What are the benefits for the team? The worry factor goes way down. Everything in our process and in our checklist approach prevents omission and oversights.

By adopting this process, you won't lose sleep. When we have confidence, we have not overlooked any detail; that confidence is transferred to our clients.

If you weren't using this process, what would you worry about? Perhaps forgetting a risk assessment in non-investment areas like debt management or healthcare and long-term insurance? Estate planning reviews and updates is another frequently overlooked area.

SECTION IV:
Thrill Your Clients

CHAPTER 8:

Become Your Client's Point Of Power

"Preparation makes the climbing easier."
— Brandon Purnell

CLIENTS WANT TO RELY on you to meet their current and future needs. That means you need to have the bench strength of a strong team that covers a wide spectrum of their evolving needs but also provides the service continuity as the aging population of financial advisors—yes, that means you—retires. Believe me, clients and their children are thinking about it, and it's your job to plan for unforeseen disability or death and the ultimate retirement of their current financial advisor. By focusing on developing efficient systems and processes to deliver your advice to clients, they will have the confidence that

CH 8 - BECOME YOUR CLIENT'S POINT OF POWER

their needs will continue to be met.

Organizations spend many millions of dollars and countless hours on training workshops each year to solve this challenge of team building and succession planning. The goal is to unlock the *benefits* team dynamics can offer, such as better decisions, increased productivity, innovation, and greater efficiency. But often teaming seems to achieve the opposite. Few teams ever work. Instead of healthy innovation, for example, some people fight for their own ideas. And instead of camaraderie, resentment and private back-talk can run rampant.

Building your high-performing team will be the focus of this chapter. We will also reinforce two key principles I shared at the start of this book, which underpin *everything* a top advisor does in his or her practice.

1. Client-centered and coordinated
2. Client advocacy

1 – A Dysfunctional Team

One of the best ways to understand the intricacies of building a high-performing team is to contrast the team with a dysfunctional team of advisors.

Classic dysfunction occurs when a senior advisor and portfolio manager (focused on equities) have a highly capable relationship manager but bring in a successful junior portfolio manager (focused on fixed income), *thinking* that a succession plan has been accomplished. Well, it hasn't! There is no agreement in place and no plan to complement each other to work on common goals and:

- Ensure every client continues to do business with you until they die, and
- Enable your team to become the *sole provider* for all clients who are decent people and follow advice.

Here's an example of two financial advisors thinking very short-term. They wanted to form a partnership without investing enough time and money to know whether this was a viability. They are both great portfolio managers, and generate excellent investment returns for clients, but they didn't work through steps 1-5:

1. Business Planning – Looking at the numbers and developing a "Formula for a Profitable Practice." Establishing goals for each core function of the business and involving each team member in implementation.

2. Team Effectiveness and Efficiency – Improving team dynamics to increase communication effectiveness and productivity.

3. Defining roles and responsibilities to capitalize on the strengths of team members.

4. Business optimization and leveraging the combined business to its maximum value.

5. Partnership Viability – Objective analysis of the pros and cons of joining forces with another advisor(s).

The classic mistake is that FAs have formed a partnership without discussing any of points 1-4. They went straight to step 5.

They are marketing the partnership to their clients but haven't discussed how to fund the marketing budget. There are no decision-making processes in place, and they have no team vision. Finally, the partnership does not have one number assigned to all clients and according to Bill Good [9] *"The model of 'ours, yours, and mine' is not a model that long survives. The reason is very simple. 'Ours' never gets the attention of 'mine' and 'yours.' "Our" clients get neglected for the simple reason that it's always easier for you to make more money by talking to 'your' clients than 'our' clients. There is no economic reason for this model to survive, and very rarely does it last more than a year or two."*

---

9 Good, Bill. "Ten Mistakes in Team Building." ThinkAdvisor. July 26, 2011. Accessed February 04, 2018. http://www.thinkadvisor.com/2011/07/26/ten-mistakes-in-team-building.

Since the partnership is formed, clients are informed, and support teammates are struggling to help. An external coach/consultant is needed desperately before more damage is done, and it all blows up, leaves a bad taste in everyone's mouth, and fractures relationships.

What's missing? Communication with the relationship manager. *Deferring to the relationship manager is key to understanding the dysfunction.*

Why? Two reasons. Number one, relationships and communication are their expertise. They are naturally attuned to people, whereas it is not the specialty of portfolio managers.

The second reason: relationship managers are typically non-financial in nature, and so aren't often given a voice as to how to fix the dysfunction. Including them demonstrates advocacy of your team. Again, the pivotal word here is *advocacy.*

The relationship manager of this partnership will play the critical role of keeping the clients happy and will offer the best chance to bring in a coach/consultant to deal with the missed steps of 1-4.

The example I just cited applies to an internal team. But external teams can be dysfunctional as well. My team was the "relationship manager" for a $6-million client turning 70 ½, and we had a "collaborative" planning process developed for the external advisors around the required minimum distribution of $2 million in retirement assets with an external portfolio manager.

CH 8 - BECOME YOUR CLIENT'S POINT OF POWER

The estate planning attorney, the CPA, and my team had to shift from a collaborative process to a client "advocacy" position because we could not get the external portfolio manager to work with us or "play nicely."

The client was well informed and watched the CPA and my team attempt to collaborate and coordinate a strategy for our mutual client's benefit. The external manager would not copy the team on emails, would not travel 30 minutes for face-to-face meetings, and would not respect deadlines or requests for information.

After several "client advocacy" attempts to coordinate the planning process from my office and the CPA, the client fired the external portfolio manager.

II - A Highly Functional Team

What can you and a functional team do for clients that they can't do for themselves? We can offer a virtual family office and a "team approach" best practice delivering client-centric strategies and coordinating them across their entire portfolio and internal and external advisors.

Here's how it is all structured. The core team is coordinated by the *Gatekeeper/Alpha Advisor* (I'll cover that in the next section of this chapter and how you can become that Gatekeeper/Alpha Advisor) and consists of involved asset custodians, family members, trustees, foundation employees, a CPA, investment managers, and estate/personal attorneys. The core team of advisors meets annually to identify family issues and concerns, develop strategies, and review progress toward solutions.

Specifically, I have acted as the Gatekeeper or Alpha Advisor (business development manager). The Gatekeeper or Alpha Advisor provides oversight and coordination of portfolio implementation, independent investment manager selections, and the asset custodian activity.

The Gatekeeper is the mastermind behind moving all the pieces in his or her internal team, and the client's team, for realizing the client's vision and goals.

Let me give you a personal example of a client of mine so you can understand how this situation can play out. For the purposes of this case study, we'll call them "the Black Family." In the room were Mr. and Mrs. Black; their unmarried children were not involved.

CH 8 - BECOME YOUR CLIENT'S POINT OF POWER

However, we have provided this service for over a decade and have set a foundation to easily insert the next generation when Mr. and Mrs. Black are ready. In addition, at my suggestion, Mr. and Mrs. Black's other financial advisors, a selected investment manager, estate attorney, and CPA are sitting at the conference table.

This annual family meeting, has over the past decade, been held in three different states to accommodate the client's needs and advisors.

The relationship manager has coordinated the logistics of the participants, the preparation of the agenda and the assignment of tasks for the prep including assignment of the discussion leader for the topic.

Some advisors calling into the meeting provide updates on investment, property insurance, and Irrevocable Life Insurance Trust (ILIT) as well as change-of-state residency and property damage updates.

The CPA will cover realized gain and losses and resulting income tax projections along with a review of the Charitable Foundation matters.

The portfolio manager will handle the hiring and firing of investment managers and the review of client fees.

The business development manager will incorporate additional advisors as needed for the changing needs of the client.

This family meeting was designed and facilitated for the client, and it helped to uncover the family's vision, values, and governance structure. We provided transparency

A TRUSTED FINANCIAL ADVISOR

regarding the coordination of the strategies involving the investments, and taxes and assets protection strategies delivered by the family's other trusted advisors.

Mr. and Mrs. Black were fully engaged in the process and asked the advisors various questions based on the content they each shared.

For many years, I have facilitated these types of meetings for clients. In many of those sessions, I have observed the interaction between family and advisors, and advisors with advisors. In the Black family meeting, an observation I had noted before became quite evident. Not only was the meeting of tremendous value to the family and designed primarily with the family in mind, but it was of equal value for the family's advisors; it was perfect for all the advisors who participated.

The advisors demonstrated their value to the Blacks and other advisors while learning more about what really mattered most to the couple. This all happened in one meeting, in one location, in one day!

Is it an expensive day for the Black family to have all their advisors in one meeting? Absolutely! Does it require a lot of planning, preparation, and coordination? Absolutely!

I would like to highlight that this effort *thrills* the client and builds a high level of trust with them. The magic occurs when the relationship manager is preparing the agenda, and the client has a chance to exercise control and ensure the focus remains on important and relevant issues.

The CPA is prepped with current portfolio return data and can prepare projections for effective tax planning.

The client enjoys seeing and hearing their team collaborate, coordinate, and plan implementation in real time.

Due to the level of preparation, the CPA can look within their organization and leverage their firm resources illustrating their branding, depth, and resources to benefit the client.

In some cases, the CPA may bring in another team member with specialty expertise to benefit the client and increase their firm's billable hours.

I have concluded over the years that what *thrills* clients and saves everyone time and resources is the efficiency of preparation and sharing a set of relevant facts once. This applies to working with insurance agents, attorneys, sports agents and investment/portfolio managers. Because once the fact set is cast, the advisory team member can collaborate and tailor their strategy offering and presentation to make it most relevant and effective.

Advisors need to understand the core components of designing and running a successful family meeting. First, you should <u>view the entire family as the client</u>, even if your relationship is with the parents or the patriarch who may have asked for the meeting.

A primary goal of any family meeting is to address the themes that matter most to the entire family; otherwise, one person's agenda may be forced onto others. Besides, no one family member holds the entire family story.

View the entire family as the client.

Second, to ensure you know what is most important to the entire family, you should speak to every family member before writing the agenda. There may be an exception to this rule: When Dad or Mom want to get their children together, so they can communicate something specific (e.g., we are selling the business). Although one can call this a family meeting, it is more akin to the "parents' meeting" for the rest of the family.

III – How to Become the Gatekeeper

If you haven't already realized, you need an introduction to the advisory team that isn't necessarily on your team, but that has been engaged by the client separate to your practice. How else are you going to influence and coordinate the process? It only takes one member of the team (external or internal to your practice) to be misaligned and throw out your hopes of coordinating your client-centered strategy.

Your introduction helps with three things:

1. Staying coordinated and executing your anticipatory approach.
2. Building a network because you are going to be asked for advisors you can refer.
3. Becoming the *Gatekeeper* for all your clients' affairs. That is, the one who the client reaches out to first anytime they have a question to ask or a need they can't resolve.

What does this ultimately do for your client? It helps them stay on course with goals and dreams, and it gives them peace of mind that everything they can't do for themselves, is being properly attended to by others.

Let me give you an example of what you don't want, and why getting introduced to the advisory team is so important for you, your client and other advisors on the client's team. I entered into a relationship with several other brokerage firms the client was not happy with; the client had some poor performing assets and estate planning concerns.

I got involved. And the first question I asked was, "How are you handling the fees?" The CPA said, "What fees?" *That's bad news.* It makes the CPA look ill-prepared. You don't want to embarrass the CPA in the meeting. What you want is to have the specifics figured out beforehand, so the CPA can help in finding answers to the following questions

- "Are we going back and filing amendments?"
- "Are we going to just pick up the fees going forward?"
- Are we going to just let the fees go?
- "Where do you pay the fees from? The taxable account? The retirement account?"

Being informed of these issues positions you as the client's advocate. Because you did the prep work with the CPA beforehand, it makes him/her look like the advocate, too.

What does it do for your practice? Builds advocacy for your brand resulting in a stream of potential clients you can choose to work with or not work with. You choose.

The questions for the attorney surrounding the estate planning were similar. Who filed the Form 709 Gift Tax return; who drafted the trust documents, and who is overseeing the annual compliance process?

The first question we need to ask ourselves is: how do we get introduced to the advisory team? Simple. Tell the clients they are getting free service. I say, "I'd like to attend

CH 8 - BECOME YOUR CLIENT'S POINT OF POWER

the next meeting. You will not get a bill from me." How do you look in the client's eyes already? You're advocating for them; you're helpful, and billing for your time isn't your primary focus.

Casually, you can ask the client about their other advisors. Whether that is the CPA, attorney, insurance agent, etc. Simply ask, "Would you (Mr./Mrs. Client), recommend this other advisor?"

If they say no, what do we want to know? <u>"Why not?"</u> You are already affecting an anticipatory approach. You already know what the client wants and aren't getting from the other advisor. That knowledge is power. Because if you can work with the team (or in the future, recommend another advisor) to fill that need, you're already stepping into the position of Gatekeeper.

If the client says yes, then you ask, "What do you like about them?" This is empowering knowledge, too. Why? Because from time to time you are going to be asked for a referral, whether it is for a CPA, attorney, insurance agent or the like. If your client advocates for their CPA, and the work they do checks out, you want to refer other clients to their CPA. When you do that, how do you look to that CPA? You're suddenly *his/her* advocate, too!

Your status elevates in a matter of moments.

Is this risky business? Some might say so. But a lot of people when asked for referrals, show the client a list of three CPAs or three attorneys and say, "You choose, Mr./Mrs. Client." That's not value-add at all. You aren't helping the client do what they can't do for themselves. And in this case, they want to make an executive decision on a CPA or attorney. *That's not the way to build a network that's going to advocate for your brand and your client.*

But I get it. I just opened a can of worms, didn't I? Don't want the competition in the room do we? I'm saying that you do. The CPA firm might offer investment advice or sell financial products like retirement plans or annuities. The private banker or the insurance agent might offer investment products. Their attorney or any of the above might question your value proposition and your fees.

I am suggesting you always discount your fees to show your appreciation, and that you always provide more value than you are charging in fees, so you are congruent around the idea your fees are reasonable and a significant value to your client.

If your client says, "Yes," the next step is to enable an introduction and then set an appointment with the advisor, whether CPA or attorney. In that meeting you are going to find out the following:

1. Are they accepting new clients?

2. More about their practice, what they do, and who they are (regardless if their answer to the previous question was "yes" or "no.").

3. How they charge. Is it by project or hourly? That's important when you make a referral. Because you don't want a client, who is expecting a project fee to be hit with a per-hour fee. You want to do the prep work beforehand.

CH 8 - BECOME YOUR CLIENT'S POINT OF POWER

What does that information allow you to do? Say your client has a need for a CPA. They come to you for a recommendation. That recommendation is worth $1,000 to a CPA. The client then calls you up and says, "That CPA just charged me $1,500 to do my taxes."

What position do you take in response? "You got off pretty cheap. Let's look at your taxes. How much are you paying in taxes? This CPA is working very hard for you to reduce that amount and for only a fraction of the cost."

If you are supportive of the CPA (and any other advisors, you have connected with and qualified) what are they going to think? Highly of you. Be their advocate. Be the client's advocate.

This tack pays off in other ways, too. As they say, "If you want to get them, you got to give them." Advocate for them, and they will advocate for you.

I was in a meeting where we were establishing a gifting trust, and the CPA said, "We are making a $15,000 annual gift for three people. We have to compound the money, and Mark Purnell is going to do a good job."

I just had to sit back and let the CPA do the talking. His talk is building my business. You can bet he's talking even when I'm not there to listen. *That's the kind of network you want to build. That's how you become the Gatekeeper.*

Once you know what's important to the client, every action involves *advocating* for all involved. Do that, and everyone gets to have a party. The one at the center making all of it possible is *you*.

I had this conversation last night with a retired professional athlete going through a divorce without a prenup. Guess who he's called? He's talking to me. I'm not a lawyer. But he's talking to me because I'm the Gatekeeper. The client comes to you with any issues first.

Now, other advisors *think of you* when they are asked for referrals because you have demonstrated you think of them.

The fact is, by practicing advocacy, by focusing on coordinating the process and remaining client-centered, you become the one who knows everyone so well that you enter their thoughts daily, and in a positive manner.

You eliminate the idea that you are the competition in the other advisors' minds. You eliminate the competition in the client's mind. Because they don't perceive there is another option besides you. *That's empowering.*

CH 8 - BECOME YOUR CLIENT'S POINT OF POWER

IV – Turn Foes to Advocates: Turn Woes to Fortune

Often, things go wrong. Often, you are serving a client, and they don't have coordinated strategies meeting their goals. So, how do you turn it around? How do you do so in a way that everyone (mostly) can win and come out of it happy?

Earlier in this chapter, I mentioned that several brokerage firms had been invited to look at how they could help the client. I quickly perceived the typical competitive situation was developing and that the firms were posturing and positioning to propose on 100% of the client's business.

I began to see the opportunity to provide advisory team leadership and become the client's Gatekeeper. In doing so, I could sit on the same side of the table with the client and talk about how we could all best serve the client.

By listing all the services that were needed and determining who was interested in and capable of providing those services one firm bowed out. Under my leadership, we then began to focus on the client's vision of success, not the advisors.

It also became obvious I was acting inclusive and advocating for my once-rival firm, and then professional courtesy and mutual respect reappeared. The client and everyone else in the room was thrilled.

Is it possible to turn rivals into fans? I say, "Yes!"

A TRUSTED FINANCIAL ADVISOR

A similar instance occurred when a population of my self-employed clients failed to have their ERISA plans updated and were identified as being out-of-compliance.

The CPA and attorneys pointed fingers at the investment firm, and the plan custodian and the client (the trustee) was upset at the entire team of advisors citing "I am paying you guys/girls to handle this stuff."

As the Gatekeeper/Alpha Advisor, I stepped into the communication void that had quickly developed. I stopped the finger pointing and coordinated and funded a strategy (engaged an ERISA attorney) to bring the plans into compliance, lobbied for amnesty, and established a plan to control any further exposure to the client and their plan.

The clients were thrilled that I shared their vision of a compliant plan and that their interest was at the center of a coordinated plan involving the collaboration of their advisors. Once again, foes were turned to advocates because pointing fingers was not the solution that was sought. Instead, their help and guidance were requested to benefit a mutual client. Result...everyone kept their job!

Once again, is it possible to turn foes into fans? I say, "Yes!"

CHAPTER 9:

How To Thrill Your Clients Time After Time

*"Live Simple...
Dream Big...
Laugh Lots...
Be Amazing."*
– Unknown

I HAVE BEEN THRILLED TO serve many wonderful clients and their families. They have welcomed me into their homes for dinner, and to stay overnight or the weekend. I have been invited to Major League Baseball spring training in both Florida's Citrus League and Arizona's Grapefruit League.

Clients became friends, and we were blessed to enjoy celebrations and accomplishments including marriages, retirements and in some special cases, life memorials. Our closeness and trust have stemmed from a shared vision formed during our performance review and investment planning sessions.

I recall some very special moments involving major life events that were incorporated into our holistic planning process.

The first is a case about early retirement. Fifteen years ago, one late afternoon, I received a call from the spouse of a 52-year-old corporate executive who owned a minority share in a private firm. I was invited to travel 90 miles for dinner the next evening.

After accepting the invite, I asked what was going on, and was informed that her highly-stressed husband needed to retire immediately and to figure out how to accelerate their retirement plan by about 10 years, without disrupting their intentions to send their kids to college or selling their home. The clients were thrilled that I canceled whatever I was doing and rearranged my calendar to meet their needs.

It's been close to 15 years; the children are debt-free college graduates and live a multiple-home lifestyle that includes a mountain home on a major ski resort. The plan we put in place that night has survived the financial crisis of 2008, and their financial advisor has enjoyed holding their annual review at their ski home during winter getaways.

The second example concerns the sale of a lake home.

A TRUSTED FINANCIAL ADVISOR

Imagine an unfamiliar boat appears at your private lake home dock and being made an offer to buy your home that is not for sale, for far more than your home is worth.

The potential buyer explains that you have the only lake parcel that will fit their dream house and they need to start the demolition of your home in the next few weeks to meet their builder's construction timetable for completion.

Once you return to your patio and relay what just happened to your spouse, you pick up the phone, call your financial advisor and ask, "Can you put these facts into our investment plan and let us know what you think in the next few days?"

I was flattered, honored and then I put their project on the top of my things to do, rolled up my sleeves and worked on a solution. A few hours of work and getting back to them with my analysis before the promised delivery date allowed me to show how important they are to me as a client.

They particularly were thrilled that I interacted with them in more than one scenario and gave them some choices. Clients love the opportunity to consider more than one option. It enables them to reach decisions with greater confidence because they have considered more than one scenario.

Several months later, when I toured their newly-constructed smaller home in a nearby community, I felt a high level of professional satisfaction knowing I'd given them

CH 9 - HOW TO THRILL YOUR CLIENTS TIME AFTER TIME

the confidence to make such an impactful financial decision in a very short period of time.

I have been blessed and proud to work with phenomenal human beings and have found a high degree of professional satisfaction in providing clients with more choices and a higher level of confidence in making their life decisions.

How do you thrill your clients sustainably? Well, you may have guessed...it all depends. There is no one-size-fits-all in this business. And if you have read the previous chapters and understand the customization needed to implement client-centered and coordinated strategies, you would laugh at the thought of there being just <u>one way</u> to achieve this goal.

However, some guidelines are useful to inform what you do for your clients, and what you do not. Think of using them as a *way of thinking* that goes behind thrilling your clients. For example, the following principles still apply:

- Do for the clients what they can't do for themselves.
- Adopt the client's vision and goals as if they were your own.
- Anticipate your client's needs and do your research beforehand.
- Advocate for the community, your client, their advisors, and everyone else involved.

Do the above four, and not only will it help you thrill your clients, but your clients will rave about you, and you will have created the opportunities to grow your client-base on demand. That's what we want, isn't it? Of course!

Let's extend the principles we have discussed, to include the following:

- **Little gestures that make big differences.** You're in the business of advising and serving your clients' interests. You're not necessarily there to entertain. Many people miss how *significant* small gestures can be for their clients.

- **How to navigate *changes* that may freak out your clients in the short-term.** Unless you explain the facts, and how they will benefit in the long-term, big opportunities don't always please clients. They can sometimes scare them because they don't have the experience. Your job is to manage that.

CH 9 - HOW TO THRILL YOUR CLIENTS TIME AFTER TIME

I – The Simplest Way to Thrill Clients

If you recall, the relationship manager's role is to maintain open, truthful, and useful communication with all stakeholders. Whether this is the hat you wear (or would like to wear for that matter), as a relationship manager, you can do a *few* simple things to thrill clients.

The first gestures concern frequent and consistent correspondence tailored to the clients' preferred mode of communication. Email or snail mail can address:

1. When the office is closed around holidays
2. Birthdays
3. "Thank you" notes for referrals
4. Condolences
5. Congratulations
6. Get well
7. Goodwill messages

Now, you might think this doesn't amount to much benefit to the client. But the more you genuinely take an interest in their affairs, over time, the more you become part of the family. Human brains are association-creating machines. If two or more events happen simultaneously, the brain decides they are *related*. How they are related depends on how you are perceived. When you consistently show up as the advisor at important events, both celebratory or grave in nature, clients create the following associations:

**My Advisor Is Always Present When Things Matter
My Advisor Is *Thinking* of Me
My Advisor Appreciates Me
My Advisor Celebrates Me**

Therefore:

1. When events of importance occur, your name comes to mind. They think of you.

2. When your name is brought to their attention, they consider it to be of importance. Simply put, you matter.

Gradually, the picture they paint of their lives and the people *in* their lives includes you more and more. The two things become inseparable. Over the years, I have realized when you make the time for others; they make the time for you. That sort of relationship is *priceless*.

This is especially true, in a day and age where attention is scarce, and connection can often be short-lived. Subsequently, you want to build bonds that matter. Building those bonds takes time. It is not done by big gestures, but by frequent gestures of sincere and good-willed intention.

Next, think of sending the client information on *their* interests. Clients want to hear from their advisors. They want to know what's going on in the markets. They want to know about upcoming financial decisions they need to make. Remember, they expect the advisory team to be <u>anticipatory</u>.

They may want to know more about retirement planning, estate planning, and education funding. Correspon-

CH 9 - HOW TO THRILL YOUR CLIENTS TIME AFTER TIME

dence doesn't have to be finance-related. They might want to know of opportunities and causes to support that align with their philanthropic interests. You could send them the latest college and career statistics because they are interested in what colleges to send their teenagers to—who are exploring career opportunities.

But clients also want to know their advisor is about more than just numbers. They want an advisor who is warm, caring, and trustworthy. That's why your letters should be a blend of financial and feel-good topics (major holidays are great for this).

The only way to consistently nurture the relationship in this manner is by sending frequent, written communications. I know you're probably thinking: *will a newsletter do the job*? No, it won't. It's better than nothing, but too many of the newsletters I've seen are overly cute, slick, and canned.

There's nothing personal about newsletters You aren't telling the client they are special and mean a lot to you. You are noting nothing specific to each client's interests.

As an exercise, write a letter to your client as if they weren't a client, but a *human being*. What would you want to tell them? What's important for them to know? What's important for you to share?

I'm not saying to write in a romantic fashion and cross the line of professionalism. Not at all. I'm talking about adding a *professionally personal touch*. Human beings are emotional beings. You can't forget that. You must respect that emotions matter.

II – A Great Advisor Helps Clients Navigate Change Successfully

I'm not here to give investment advice. In fact, I won't. Specific investment advice doesn't necessarily stand the test of time anyway. But what I can share, is a way of thinking that you can adapt to help develop proven success strategies *through* the times. This is something the portfolio manager and relationship manager both want to consider when developing strategies that thrill clients.

The question is, how do you move from a *known* proven success strategy to one we hope will take us *beyond* our previous possibilities?

In my career, I have had two pivotal periods necessitating major change or transformation. The first involved my decision to convert $20 million in legacy mutual fund positions to an advisory program, and the second involved a Funnel #3 growth strategy that was wildly successful (I share more about this in the next chapter).

Throughout the 1980s s and early 1990s, many of my clients invested in class A mutual fund shares. Their strategy was to hold for long-term growth and making changes to their holdings were limited to other funds within the fund family. Clients assumed I was continuing to manage that fund and watch it, and I would make recommendations to change that investment over time.

Well, that was not the case at all. I had an advisory process to accomplish that, but it wasn't relevant to what the clients owned. The clients had paid a placement fee many

CH 9 - HOW TO THRILL YOUR CLIENTS TIME AFTER TIME

years prior and couldn't trade outside the mutual fund family without a trading cost.

So, I had to convert about 200 smaller accounts and move them from a stagnant investment strategy to a continual discretionary management process.

Why advisory? To succeed in complex markets, you need objective, reliable advice. Sometimes, the best advice is to hold steady and maintain your investments. Other times, the best advice is to take immediate action. <u>Above all, you need advice you can trust.</u>

It can be challenging to keep abreast of the market and to continually manage and monitor your investment portfolio. With thousands of money managers, most people do not have the time or the resources to perform the necessary due diligence and analysis on the investments for their portfolio or to perform the necessary analysis to build a portfolio in the first place—rather than a collection of investments.

Advisory accounts give investors the opportunity to:

- Consult with an investment professional.

- Receive advice on security selection and portfolio construction.

- Buy and sell securities for their portfolios without paying a commission for the trades. An annual fee (billed quarterly in advance), based on assets, is charged in most advisory accounts.

As part of the advisory process, the financial advisor works with clients to determine the right asset allocation for their risk tolerance and investing timeframe, and will regularly monitor the account, rebalancing when necessary to maintain the proper allocations.

This involves guiding clients through a four-step process for defining, developing, implementing, and monitoring their personalized portfolio-management plan.

The Advisory Process

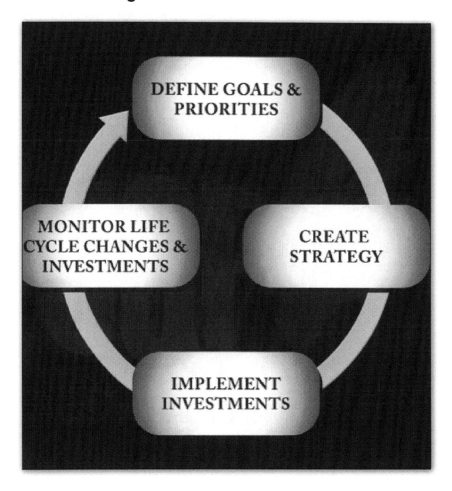

CH 9 - HOW TO THRILL YOUR CLIENTS TIME AFTER TIME

Assuming you have a clear understanding of your client's goals and priorities, you would need to develop a strategy that helps them fulfill those aims. I had to show the strategy to the clients because it would make our working relationship more efficient. And I would make sure they could understand me.

If you recall, that's one of the key things a good portfolio manager can do. They can communicate in simple terms, what the client couldn't possibly understand for themselves. Again, we are doing for the client what they can't do for themselves.

In my example, I needed to illustrate to the clients many benefits of the "new" process. The first implication was simple: You prefer someone manage your assets for a fee rather than managing them yourself.

Next, I needed to show the client it would benefit them to pay a larger management fee to have the advisor cover both management *and* trading costs. I said something along the lines of: *"This benefit is most likely realized if you believe that a strategy with more trading is effective for both investment performance and the fact that you wouldn't directly be covering the trading commissions."*

Third, be aware of what's called "reverse churning," and the potential conflict of interest. If the advisor is footing the bill for trades but is charging the client a wrap fee, the advisor has an incentive to trade the client's accounts less to limit their expenses and earn higher profits.

Now, I would tend to agree that limited trading or limiting costs, in general, is practice for investment performance, but if this is what you believe, you might consider whether you're better off not paying a wrap fee and just paying the trading commissions yourself. I believe it's important for investment advisors to limit conflicts of interest where they may arise, and this structure can promote more complications.

Fourth, I educate clients on the usefulness of a household performance report including various accounts and sub-account performance to be provided on a quarterly basis to document their progress.

Lastly, I let clients know that if they do engage in a wrap fee arrangement with an advisor, at their annual checkup they should review the effectiveness to see how it is faring. To do this, they need to determine the fee they would have paid for each trade and multiply it by the number of trades in each category.

This simple analysis gives clients a clear view of either the premium or discount they are receiving through the program. It will also be worth evaluating in the context of their investment performance.

An asset-based fee positions the client to see their fee in dollar terms that will increase and decrease as the accounts fluctuate.

I would have to train my teammates, educate the client and learn the nuances of the strategy because, in turn, it would make me more efficient and give the client what they thought they were already getting. It would make me more efficient in working with a larger number of clients. It made sense to develop a transition plan.

CH 9 - HOW TO THRILL YOUR CLIENTS TIME AFTER TIME

How does one get from one book of business to another without destroying their revenue stream or creating unintended consequences for their client?

This is when I consider myself **DISTURBED**. I am not satisfied I am not producing a holistic approach, or that investment product limitations will prevent me from meeting the client needs and delivering a fully client-centered strategy.

III – D-I-S-T-U-R-B-E-D

Welcome to DISTURBED, an acronym for a methodology to effect change:

- **DISCOVERY** (Is it a good fit?)
- **INVESTIGATE** (Check out references)
- **STRATEGY** (Sometimes referred to as proposal)
- **TEST THE STRATEGY** with conditions and low-risk outcomes; (dip your toe in the water but don't jump in)
- **UNCONDITIONAL COMMITMENT** (Jump in with both feet)
- **REMEMBER** and celebrate your successes.
- **BELIEVE** and **BUILD** on this transformation.
- **EVALUATE** and prepare for the next transition.
- **DESIGN** the next discovery session.

This technique is designed to cause transformational change without disrupting your existing business revenue stream. It is also designed to help your clients make transformational changes, without disrupting their goals and visions.

Discovery

With every opportunity to effect change for a client, you must first discover if you have a good fit. Why? You want to know that you can fulfill the client's objectives. And, you want to know that serving this client will be beneficial to your practice, too. I discussed this consideration in a previous chapter; at times, you will have to learn to say no.

First, discover if an opportunity is a good fit. In the previous example, I couldn't make changes to the client's portfolio if it involved a mutual fund outside their current fund family. I had been in practice for about 10 years, and clients expected me to make recommendations and review the holdings. I had to go out and make some discoveries to see if Advisory Process B would be a good fit for my client and whether it would work over the long-term.

To use a baseball analogy, it'd be like changing my pitch selection, so instead of throwing a hard curveball, I would throw a slider, a ball that would only move a little. I did some discovery to see if this new strategy would work for me and whether it would work for my clients.

Once I found out whether it would be a good solution for the client, and an apt solution for many clients in a similar situation, then I could do some real digging. I could run it past a few people and identify if it would work. This where the next step of the DISTURBED methodology comes in.

Investigate

I would certainly do some research and see if, in fact, other advisors had made this decision. If anybody had written on the topic and any research was available, I could talk to other advisors who might have already performed this transition. *Was there any data available? I had to investigate.*

Strategy

Your next step is to obtain a strategy. You must get a proposal. I want to develop a strategy defining how am I going to help clients make a transition. Are these clients going to need to come into the office?

I'll take their statement and write a note on it that says, "Hey, you should call me right away because I've got some recommendations, and I'd like to suggest some changes."

So, I'm working on a strategy and brainstorming. How am I going to propose to make these changes? I need to move clients from **Product A** over to **Advisory Process B.**

Testing

Next, you want to test the strategy. This is where it begins to get interesting. My initial thoughts are to have a client list of 1 to 100, with 1 being the most complex client and 100 being the client with the simplest circumstances. This is important because I want to protect my client's interests and minimize the costs of absorbing/fixing any unintended consequences.

I would start with the client with the least complex financial strategy and make the change from **Product A to Advisory Process B.** The product is what I have; I want to

CH 9 - HOW TO THRILL YOUR CLIENTS TIME AFTER TIME

get them into a process, and I'm going to need to educate them about how to make that change. I could develop the strategy and aim it right to my number one client, who it would have the biggest impact on, and if I did it right, he or she are going to love me, and we could consider it a home run.

But there's a lot of moving parts in transitioning from **Product A** to **Process B**. There's risk because there's a learning curve. I'm going to have to answer questions for the client.

- "How is this new process going to work?"
- "Is it going to cost me any money?"
- "Will tax implications arise in changing from one to the other?"

Then I must answer questions for myself:

- How is my staff going to interact?
- How am I going to do the trading?

The low-risk way to proceed would be by starting with client number 100. In baseball terms, this would be hitting a single, because it's going to be less complicated and you will be less involved when using that strategy.

There's less risk because if it goes completely wrong and the client wants to fire me, it's not my number one client firing me. Again, if during the early part of the learning curve, costs arise that must be absorbed, they should be minimized. That's what I mean by low-risk. This is an effective testing strategy.

Unconditional Commitment

Again, the "U" in DISTURBED stands for an *Unconditional Commitment* to your strategy. Once I know I've tested it, I'm ready to jump in completely. Now, the results are going to be more meaningful because I'm having successes and I know how to overcome challenges. I know how to overcome objections of changing from **Product A to Process B**.

Remember & Celebrate

I want to *Remember* those successes and *Celebrate* them with the client because that's how I'm going to change my belief system that the new strategy really works. By making a conscious effort and recognizing its value, we have created a high-five "AHA" moment with the client, because we were able to improve their situation. Once again, I have peeked at the new world unfolding for my practice that will thrill my client.

Believability

As I move now from client 80 to client 1, I'm now really seeing the benefits of the transition take place and the movement of the methodology affect the change. My *Be-*

CH 9 - HOW TO THRILL YOUR CLIENTS TIME AFTER TIME

lievability is now built up. I'm improving and am sharp and efficient as I proceed.

Evaluate

The next step is to sit back and *Evaluate,* now that I've gotten the clients out of **Product A** and into **Process B.** The client knows and understands I will be monitoring the investment. I will be giving them increased benefits they didn't have before.

Previously, they had a stagnant investment product, and if it needed to be updated, it was probably not going to be a top priority because I didn't have a process in place to monitor it.

We have now become more efficient and can help greater groups of people because the process is in place, and team members are all up to speed. The training has been done; we can onboard clients faster, and into a more efficient operation.

Knowing that I've just made a change to improve my situation and the clients' situation, it's now time to evaluate other opportunities I might have. The next opportunity might be a product or a process that will enable me to have better tax control for the client.

I want to move to the next improvement we can make in the client relationship because the client is now thrilled, and we can accomplish another goal that will benefit them as well as benefit the efficiency of the practice.

Design the Next Discovery

At this point, we're evaluating; we're redesigning, and revisiting the beginning of DISTURBED in the first Discovery phase, but now, we are *designing our next discovery*. We are asking ourselves: *Is this next strategy going to be a "good fit?*

The DISTURBED process is more of a cycle. It never ends. You can use it to impact ongoing positive change. That's key. Clients don't want great results that are sporadic. They want great results that sustain.

IV – Homework: Thrill Your Clients

You have three tasks to complete.

First, craft a custom communication piece for ONE client. Make sure it is useful to them and that they will be interested in it. The piece should be personal. One of my favorite notes is: "I saw you in the press...congrats on your recent accomplishment." Then you can send a hand-written note along with a copy of the article or clipping. Once you send it, take notice of the feedback the client gives you.

Second, what's a strategy or process that works well for your clientele? Look at how you discovered, tested, and tweaked that strategy, and how much of the DISTURBED methodology you checked off unknowingly.

Third, what's a strategy or process you are interested in exploring for use with your clientele? Use the DISTURBED methodology to determine if it is worthwhile to apply it to your clientele who have similar needs.

SECTION V:
Built To Last

CHAPTER 10:

Secure Hidden Profit Streams That Are Right Under Your Nose

"Let's Harvest Your Blind Spot"
– Mark Purnell

I had a conversation with Blaine Gibson at Robert W. Baird & Co. Incorporated, a national firm with about 900 advisors. About a decade ago, they realized approximately 50% of their accounts were contributing almost nothing to the profitability of the firm, so they hired Blaine and created, what they called, a "client resource team."

This department or team of advisors oversaw developing a process that would sift through orphaned and displaced accounts to coach these accounts up to a level where the firm could add value or coach them out to another firm that would better fit their needs. The clients

CH 10 - SECURE HIDDEN PROFIT STREAMS

weren't getting the service they deserved, and the firm was concerned and wanted to keep the interests of the clients a priority. I'll break down the mechanics of the process they used in this chapter, along with three other processes you can use to secure more hidden profit streams that are right under your nose. For now, let's return to discussing what Blaine shared.

Blaine called a client with a $5,000 account and tried to coach him to move his money away from the firm because they were not engaged, and in fact, the fees charged on the account were costing the client $125 a year just to keep the account with the firm.

But one of the possibilities that Blaine leveraged in their firm's process of working through these accounts was to show the client that if they could bring the account up to a certain mark, then the advisor could add value and that their current fee would be justified. In this case, they offered to the client: "If you bring the account up to $25,000, we could put you into a strategy we can better monitor and service."

Well, this particular client said, "Great. I appreciate that." And he sent in $20,000 to get the account up to $25,000. Through this engagement process, the advisor then learned that the gentleman's wife had a business that was taking off. It was only a matter of months before the clients sent in $700,000 to put into the proposed management solution and subsequently, another $400,000. Within three years, the account was $1.2 million. This was a win-win situation, and the firm was rewarded for looking after the client's best interests.

Over the last 10 years, through the process implemented by the "client resource team," the historically smaller accounts are now efficiently managed, and ROA's have increased 100bps on average. While some accounts do get coached away from the firm, the process that's put in place can garner rewards. Now, if the firm had not had the insight, the foresight, and been willing to create a counterintuitive process, those assets and revenue would be elsewhere. I wanted to share this real-life case study to demonstrate how paying attention to the bottom 5% of your book can have an impact on your practice. As a side note, the process from start to finish moves the client in one way or another within 4-6 months. Imagine your "C" book of business achieving a high level of efficiency in 4-6 months.

The above example is just <u>one</u> of <u>four</u> streams of profit that are right under your nose. Let's get to discussing all four, so you can maximize the value you provide to your client-base, and subsequently, maximize your practice's income streams.

I – The 80/20 Rule

Since I started working with and learning from Bill Good, a thought leader for financial advisors for over 40 years, my business and life have changed. It is important to call him out for his accomplishments, and I thank him for his early research in this area.

If you were to list your clients from 1-100, it is very often the case that 80% of the business you do is with the top 20 of that 100. It is very frequent that the bottom half of your accounts may only make up maybe 5%, 10%, or 15% of your business.

Regarding practice efficiency, it is often considered that one should focus strictly on where 80% of your business comes from, which would be the top 20% of your clients. We must consider there are many sources of where that 20% will come from over time.

Certainly, from one year to the next, there will be some repeaters. Certainly, you are going to get referrals from this year's top 20%, and certainly, you are going to secure new clients from your existing relationships in the community. So, let's call those new clients who are not related to any of your existing clients.

But there are also two other sources—that I call the <u>bottom 80% of your clients</u>—who are now giving you 20% of your business. These are people who've invested money elsewhere, or they've recently come into some money, but you essentially only have a portion of their assets. The last component is referrals from that bottom 80%.

Common industry practice focuses on the idea of pruning your book. That means you would dismiss or move away from the clients in the bottom 20%. *That's not a wise idea in my view. I've never felt very good about it.*

I've always had the perspective that if a client wants to trust me with their money and to give them advice, then I should honor that, and I should work with them. Perhaps I shouldn't take on more clients if I don't feel I can do that. However, every professional must make that decision on their own.

If you cut off the bottom 80% of your clients, then clearly, you have just eliminated many possible referral sources, and many possibilities for that bottom 80% to move up and graduate into the top 20% of your clients. The bottom 80% will give you the four hidden profit streams!

For our conversation going forward, I'm going to refer to and create four funnels. It's important to be able to identify these funnels and pipelines and know that you can track and measure your activities. You can plan what I'll call *drip marketing techniques* into these various funnels.

What's drip marketing? It is a communication strategy that sends or drips a pre-written or predetermined set of messages to customers or prospects over time. These messages often take the form of email, but they can apply to any other medium. It could be snail mail. It can be a combination of all the platforms.

When using a pre-written set of messages, we can start to cultivate the funnels, and either convert them to bigger client accounts, moving them from one funnel to another or; we can clear them out because there is genuinely nothing we can do for them.

Funnel #1

Funnel number one will be used with the clients who are in the existing top 20 needing additional services. Imagine that you only have, again, some of their assets. How do we cultivate that top 20 to increase your business and your penetration in working with them and doing a better job for them?

You want to develop a campaign in a financial service area you are not serving but where you could provide interest. You could showcase you have expertise in another area. A good example of that would be in the credit/lending area.

Most financial advisors will work with a client's assets and their liabilities, but they tend to focus more on their assets. If your clients are using credit and borrowing money through credit cards, home mortgages, and business loans, however, they're creating debt; you could begin to drip on those clients with an expertise or an availability to help them.

You know what interest rate they're paying. Maybe you can get a better interest rate or terms. That's one way to cultivate funnel one.

Funnel #2

These clients typically have substantial external assets, and the reason is that these are existing clients in your bottom 80%, but they have the potential to move up to the top 20. These clients are very good candidates to be in the top 20. You must figure out what services they are obtaining elsewhere that they could obtain from you and your firm.

The education, and again, the drip campaign that you would develop messaging for identifies areas and highlights your expertise and firm resources they're not using to their advantage.

An example might be retirement assets. Let's say a client has their retirement assets elsewhere, whether at the firm where they are currently working or with another firm. Demonstrate expertise and knowledge in the area that the retirees must deal with, and then they can see, "Oh, this is something that you are offering." They can understand how they might take advantage of your services and consolidate with you. *This is how the clients will move up from the bottom 80 to the top 20.*

Concerning retirement assets, how would you convert them? You could look at your planning work and seek to reduce the risk on the overall portfolio by collaborating and having the vision to see that you can coordinate these two pools of money; the assets held outside (external assets), and those held internally. To top it off, when assets are typically consolidated, there might be an opportunity to reduce fees, and certainly, your client would be open to that.

Funnel #3

This funnel applies to prospects, advocates of yours in the community, and client advisors. You might find a good example of an advocate in an area where you have an interest. They might be in the arts community, a religious community; it might be in a trade area. If you work with dentists, advocates might be in their trade association. They might be found through a community effort like Save the Library, your local college or universities. If it's a subject you are interested in, and these people know you because you work actively in the interest, they could become an advocate.

To fill funnel number three, identify your ideal client, ideal assets or desired assets under management, their family makeup, what industry they work in, what concerns them, their professions, common problems, marital/relationship status, and their referral sources resulting from their personal circumstances.

Based on that information, we cultivate them. We demonstrate interest in the philanthropic or in the arts community if that's one of the areas where you're focused. We get engaged in programs where your ideal clients are also aligned and interested, and offer to help, learn, and collaborate with these entities to assist them in solving problems.

To convert them into higher paying customers, you must be alert to the opportunities because they come quickly. You can assume leadership positions, volunteer for speaking time or to obtain or secure speakers. You could offer to fund a program using your DAF and that could help you fund any of these activities requiring funding.

Funnel #4

Funnel number four ties back into the industry examining what we'll call the bottom 5% or 10% of your client base. *This is a real hidden income stream for the advisor.* When you consider, in many firms, the bottom 5% or 10% don't have any real impact I would suggest you consider pruning the smaller, less productive clients in your book of business that others think aren't worth the effort.

How do you cultivate this income stream that's right under your nose? First, you need to develop a process, as Blaine has done. Let the process guide you through your client interactions. You will need to know what you are doing with them as a team, and who in your team is going to do what.

First, your process must demonstrate that you appreciate your client for working with you and that you recognize for some reason; their relationship has fallen below your service level. Remember, your process needs to epitomize your client's best interests.

Second, you must analyze the client relationship and coach the client to a better option. You might be coaching them to leave the firm and to get the service they need and deserve. That would be one aspect of the process.

Third, you also need to figure out a way to contact those clients because many times, they aren't going to be responsive since you haven't been interacting with them regularly. So, 1) you need to figure out how you're going to contact them to have the conversation, and 2) you will be able to contact and speak to them.

Last, if leaving your firm isn't in their best interests, you must identify what would be needed to take this client to a minimum service level they could receive from your team and you. In Blaine's example, the account might have $5,000 in it; then you have an opportunity to provide a basic minimum service if they brought the account up to $25,000 or $50,000. Your process should identify and explain this plan to them.

Capitalizing on Change

The 80% of your business coming from 20% of your clients *will* change over time. It will change because clients' needs change. Clients are going to die. Clients from the top 20 will spend their money. They could transfer accounts out. There are many reasons why this aspect of your business will shift, and my experience has been, over a 30-year career, that clients could move from the bottom 5% and 10% (Funnel #4) and travel through these funnels over the course of a career.

This shouldn't come as a surprise to you since we covered trends across the generations in Chapter 1. Remember, over the coming decades, massive amounts of wealth will be transferred from the silent and baby boomer generations to Gen X, and so forth.

With the four funnels I discussed in place, you can track these changes over time, and be *anticipatory* to clients' needs. Again, you and your team can prepare to serve clients' needs well before they even recognize they have them. What does this demonstrate to clients? You are looking out for their lives.

CHAPTER 11:

The Success Mindset Every Trusted Advisor Needs

*"Give a man a fish, and you feed him for a day.
Teach a man to fish, and you feed him for a lifetime."*
– Chinese Proverb

BRANCH MANAGERS CAN BE a great partner for financial advisors. They can draw on a wide array of resources. All the good ones have systems and processes in place to help an advisor reach their full potential. Sometimes, an advisor and their branch manager must customize this systematic approach to design and develop client-centric solutions.

In 2007, I began to work with my branch manager and regional staff on my vision of delivering a "holistic" client-centered strategy that I could collaborate and coordi-

CH 11 - THE SUCCESS MINDSET

nate with my client's advisors. I was also concerned and consulted with my CPA on "The Business Development Budget" and how the new efforts would fit into the profit formula due to the funnel marketing I had implemented nationally.

My team had developed a "Service Methodology for Sports & Entertainment Clients" in 2005, and we were having great success. The Funnel #3 strategy, which I shared with you in Chapter 9, had quickly become a significant segment of the practice and required out-of-the-box thinking for most solutions.

We were looking for every blind spot we could identify to serve our clients and to share their visions of success. We were not the custodian of all our clients' assets; we offered "a la carte pricing" for unbundled services like Investment Policy Statement, Asset Allocation Study, Investment Manager Search & Selection, and Performance Monitoring. We collaborated and coordinated the implementation of strategies with other investment firms, insurance agents, bank trust operations, CPAs, and attorneys.

The methodology we used for Sports & Entertainment clients with "small institutional" asset levels greater than $5 million was not different than what I have shared with you in this book. Our mantra was, "What can you do for these clients that they can't do for themselves?" and we used a team approach to assure our strategies were client-centered and coordinated.

The core team was coordinated by The Gatekeeper/Alpha Advisor (my team) and consisted of involved asset custodians, family members, trustees, foundation employees, a CPA, lead investment managers, and estate/personal attorneys.

Our core team of advisors met annually to identify family issues and concerns, develop strategies, and review progress toward solutions. Specifically, the Gatekeeper or Alpha Advisor provided a customized investment policy statement, established asset allocation guidelines, and monitored the progress quarterly for a hard dollar or asset-based fee. Additionally, we provided cash flow solutions, credit facilities and performed an audit and annual review of fees/implementation costs.

The Gatekeeper or Alpha Advisor continued to provide oversight and coordination of portfolio implementation, independent investment manager selections and the asset custodian activity. This decentralized approach provided (and still provides) a great deal of confidence in the engagement/termination process.

In this one instance, I wanted to continue the thread of delivering holistic advice, while meeting the demands of the branch supervisory environment, expected revenue generation, and its product limitations. Instead, the circumstances created obstacles the advisor had to find a delicate balance around.

This feeling forced me to ask myself, *is this the best place for me to serve my clients, build a career, and make a difference in this world while providing for my family?*

I was led to believe I needed to *update* the way I thought about my practice because I was confronted with a situation where my work philosophy could potentially be com-

CH 11 - THE SUCCESS MINDSET

promised. By remaining focused on the client's needs, we achieved a win/win for all involved.

By using all the resources available in an open and constructive framework, we could serve our client's needs that were atypical for our team particularly in the credit, lending, insurance and trust/foundation areas. The major hurdle we had to overcome, along with our branch supervisory staff, was our "belief system" around the idea of becoming the Gatekeeper/Alpha Advisor.

Typically, the custodian of the assets or the portfolio manager are viewed as the Alpha Advisor. Our new belief system led us to focus on a "shared client vision" centering on investment guidelines and oversight, asset allocation, and advisor team collaboration and coordination.

This situation is quite common for advisors who are very client-centered and have branch managers who may not necessarily align with their thinking. Or, who have branch managers with processes that aren't flexible enough to accommodate holistic strategies and innovative foresight.

Recently, I coached a conflicted advisor who was in the process of changing his employment situation. His career was on the decline because his strategy and methods of serving his clients weren't aligned with his firm's expectations and goals for his team. The firm wanted a higher number of phone contacts generated per day, while he wanted to practice a more involved holistic approach requiring additional time. Many advisors find themselves in this predicament.

Even though he was delivering results in the top 1% of his peer group, he was told he was underperforming because his firm wanted him to make 40 calls per day versus the 20+ daily calls he was making to reach his top-tier performance—based on assets gathered and the number of accounts opened. He's was doing well on one front, but not meeting firm expectations on another.

I say he is a top performer who's just not in the right spot. He will eventually change his beliefs about the firm and the advisory position he is in and will migrate to his natural bent of being a holistic advisor.

In the early 1980s, while I was in graduate school, I studied Robert Schuller's work[10] and incorporated it into my professional discipline. Dr. Schuller offered readers the keys to better living that have worked for him as well as other successful men and women. When following the principles of Dr. Schuller's unique Peak to Peek principle, readers learn to use peak experiences to inspire themselves to bigger and better things.

The Peak to Peek principal in its simplest form is attempting to allow your belief system, to permit you to see a new desired "Peak." By allowing your faith and actions to move you to a peak experience, you become a new person with new experiences. With new eyes, you can "Peek" and see the surprise that awaits the new you—an updated frontier of opportunities and possibilities.

---

10 Schuller, Robert Harold. The Peak to Peek Principle. New York: Bantam Books, 1990.

CH 11 - THE SUCCESS MINDSET

The inflection point is usually evidenced by one of these comments:

- "You can't do that!"
- "Nobody else has done it like that!"

If you encounter these thoughts, you might want to consider it a good sign. Why? Because it likely means you are building a practice other advisors will marvel at, one that you never thought you could build. You are building a practice that serves amazing clients and helps them through tumultuous times by providing keen and unique insight and guidance.

You will be accused of _"Marching to the beat of a different drummer."_ And, you will be on your way to "living a dream-filled life" for you and your clients. You will be on a journey, rife with realized dreams. On this journey you will hear this statement:

> *"We are going to make an exception for you because we think you are onto something."*

I - What Got You Here is Not Going to Get You There

We all must deal with making changes in our basic belief system about how we can help our clients meet their goals and objectives. It can be a refreshing and recharging process and propel you and your clients into new territories that can lead to major improvements and improved results.

Why is this an important topic for a trusted advisor? The advisor must have a strong belief that what they are providing to their clients is what they need. It's the best that can be offered, and when the strategy/process is followed, the results will be efficiently attained.

A trusted advisor must constantly challenge their existing way of thinking.

Most financial advisors are highly motivated and enterprising business people. You have had some huge successes but what got you here is not going to get you there, so get ready for some real work.

About 20 years ago, one of my coaches pulled me aside in a group environment and said the following:

> *"Mark, you are going to have the toughest job in the room moving to the next level because of all of the successes that you have enjoyed, and what you have learned is going to be obsolete and useless going forward."*

Right then, I knew I was going to have to fly differently just like the bumblebee flies differently from an airplane.

CH 11 - THE SUCCESS MINDSET

Luckily for me, I have always been open to taking on coaching and advice from mentors who have been where I want to go, mentors who can help me see my blind spots and bring them to light, so I can continue to grow myself and my practice.

II – What's Your Motivation?

As I reflect on a 30 year+ career, I ask myself **what were the driving motivations**? *How did the driving motivations contribute to my capacity to serve my clients and thrill them?*

My business was tightly geared around helping clients make better decisions about their money. That's why I got into the advisory business. The work I was doing as an advisor is what many advisors undertake to create more choices for their clients.

Your clients will, over time, become your friends, and they're going to become people who trust you immensely, and you're going to provide huge peace of mind to them. You're going to help them send their kids to attend college; you're going to help them build homes, and support their lifestyles, maybe start a business. Perhaps support their charitable interests. *That's my motivation.*

Advising was my vehicle to support people's lives and dreams.

Over the course of my journey, I realized I couldn't help everybody. I had to streamline what I was doing and become more efficient. I had to streamline what my team was able to do and that involved making some changes in the way we carried out our daily activities.

Next, I needed to develop more processes and maybe some key solutions to help the client and their families live the life they wanted.

CH 11 - THE SUCCESS MINDSET

Then, as I strengthened my conviction in my philosophy of holistic strategies centered around the clients' needs, I was confronted with the fact that not everyone had the same viewpoint—including other advisors or branch managers. While this presented challenges, it also presented *opportunities* for me to innovate and stand by my values as a professional.

In many instances, what I did failed. But I pivoted swiftly and found a solution. One that resulted in a win-win for all.

I was willing to do what others weren't to achieve results that others could only dream of.

Which leads me to where I am now, as I live out a very attractive sun-setting arrangement for my career as an advisor. Today, I'm still interested in helping families live the life they couldn't have, but I'm more focused on delivering my ideas through their advisor. That's you!

I'm passionate about wanting to help my clients make better decisions about their money. But at this stage of my career, I've decided if I can help advisors grow thriving, client-centered and coordinated practices, I could reach that many more people. That sort of impact will live far beyond my lifetime. *I want to live and leave a legacy.*

On average over my career, I've impacted about 200 households. Well, now, if I've helped 200 households, imagine if I could impact 200 advisors. Using an advisor multiplier, then I could impact 40,000 households. So, I'm looking to have a much bigger impact. If that resonates with you, and you want a more personalized mentor and coach to build the practice of your dreams, get in touch with me by booking your free strategy session at https://calendly.com/mark-purnell.

Whether we continue to work together or not, I would like to leave you with some concluding remarks and guidance for this book. Take a moment to reflect and understand your *motivation* behind doing what you do as an advisor.

You can make money in many ways. I'm going to encourage you to clarify a reason that is bigger than just what you earn, take home, and what that buys you in life. Sure, that stuff is important. I'm not belittling it.

But the easiest way to adopt a client's vision and take it as your own is to have a genuine purpose to serve life. Then you don't have to force yourself or remind yourself to take actions in the interests of your clients. Why? Because the drive is intrinsic.

Remember, the work you do as an advisor is about creating more *choices* for your clients. You also get to see people through some of their toughest challenges and transitions in life, from grieving loved ones, finding new jobs after a redundancy, or dealing with divorces. More importantly, you get to help clients come out of these events and rebuild their lives even stronger.

Advisory is about people, not numbers.

I hope this book has been insightful, enriching, and inspirational for you. In writing it, I endeavored to craft the guide I wish I'd had back in the day when I was starting out.

CH 11 - THE SUCCESS MINDSET

My wish for you is to use this book to create the life of your dreams, by helping your clients create the life of their dreams.

I wish you and your loved ones the best that life can offer!

BONUS: Free Strategy Call

You can book your FREE strategy call with Mark Purnell, valued at $300. On that call, Mark will work with you to clarify your goals and assess your needs. This could be any one or more of the following:

- GAIN high-net-wealth clients without having to spend a fortune.
- Develop WINNING strategies for your clients that aren't based on "luck," and strategies that will thrill them time after time.
- Build and SUSTAIN your practice in the short term and for the long-run.
- Secure HIDDEN profit streams that are right under your nose.
- Be THE PREFERRED ADVISOR clients and other consultants in your community think of first whenever they have a want or need.
- Turn your competition and foes into raving FANS.
- BUILD and lead a winning team of advisors.
- Get MORE done in less time.

To book your free strategy session, go to: MarkPurnell.net/bonus

I look forward to working with you to gain the BEST of what life can offer!

—Mark W. Purnell, *CIMA*

Appendix

Glossary of Terms

- **Business Development Manager (BDM):** A business development manager works to improve an organization's market position and achieve financial growth.

- **Relationship Manager (RM):** A relationship manager is a professional who works to improve a firm's relationships with both partner firms and customers.

- **Portfolio Manager (PM):** A portfolio manager is a person or group of people responsible for investing assets, implementing investment strategy, and managing day-to-day portfolio trading.

- **Silent Generation:** Born 1925-1942 (Age 67-84), these individuals were too young to see action in World War II and too old to participate in the fun of the Summer of Love. This label describes their conformist tendencies and belief that following the rules was a sure ticket to success.

- **Baby Boomers:** Born 1943-1964 (Age 48-66), the boomers were born during an economic and baby

APPENDIX

boom following World War II. These hippie kids protested the Vietnam War and participated in the civil rights movement, all with rock 'n' roll music blaring in the background.

- **Generation X:** Born 1965-1979 (Age 32-47), they were originally called the baby busters because fertility rates fell after the boomers. As teenagers, they experienced the AIDs epidemic and the fall of the Berlin Wall. Sometimes called the MTV Generation, the "X" in their name refers to this generation's desire not to be defined.

- **Millennials:** Born 1980-2000 (Age 14-34), they experienced the rise of the Internet, September 11th, and the wars that followed. Sometimes called Generation Y because of their dependence on technology, they are said to be entitled and narcissistic.

- **Generation Z:** Born 2001-2013 (Age 1-13), these kids are the first born into an Internet-established world and are suspected to be the most individualistic and technology-dependent generation. Sometimes referred to as the i-Generation.

- **Family Steward:** This is the person in the family looking out for other family members who might be a spouse, children, parents, siblings, and grandchildren. The Family Steward, in my experience, is a person looking out for all the financial interests of these individuals.

- **Profit Formula:** (Gross production of advisor/team * payout from firm) − (the Business Development Budget)
- **The Business Development Budget:** Expenses other than owner/lead advisor compensation, e.g., payroll for additional staff, charitable gifting to support client philanthropy, travel, and entertainment, etc.
- **Internal Team of Advisors:** CSA, platform support, product specialist, and lenders.
- **External Team of Advisors:** Client's CPA, attorney, banker, financial advisors, insurance agents.
- **Client's Advocate:** An advisor who adopts the client's vision, goals, and needs, as if they were their own, and commits to making sure they are fulfilled.
- **Client-Centered:** Striving to do the best job possible for clients. This also involves putting interests behind clients' and offering the most appropriate solutions. Being client-centered is more than a mental attitude and an ethical stance.
- **Client Services Associate (CSA):** A broker/sales assistant who helps financial advisors (traditionally called brokers) with time management by handling routine client inquiries, mainly those related to account maintenance matters, freeing financial advisors to devote more time to their value-added activity, and providing investment advice.

APPENDIX

- **Ideal High-Net-Worth Client:** Client who has investable assets of >$750,000 born before 1964.
- **Value Proposition:** An innovation, service, or feature intended to make your practice attractive to clients.
- **"Moment of Truth" Event:** An instance of contact or interaction between a client and a firm (through a product, sales force, or visit) that gives the client an opportunity to form or change an impression about the firm.
- **Gatekeeper:** The Gatekeeper is the leader of the client's sounding board for vetting new ideas and strategies.
- **Financial Advisor (FA)**

ABOUT MARK PURNELL

Mark Purnell is a top advisor with over 33-years of experience in the industry. He has served clients in 34 states through the USA. Mark has made <u>over 50 million dollars</u> for clients over the course of his career. But more importantly, he has provided over $400,000 to support his clients' philanthropic and charitable interests, in service to the greater community.

Today, Mark coaches and consults other financial advisors to help them build the practice of their dreams and live the life they love. And in many cases, the life they never thought possible. This book is Mark's way to give back to a profession that has been a blessing to him *and* his family. Mark graduated from the University of Wisconsin, Madison with an MBA in Finance & Investments and from Delaware State University (a member of Historically Black Colleges and Universities) with a B.S. in Accounting.

Made in the USA
Columbia, SC
18 October 2018